UNTOURIST BRISBANE

An insider guide to the best places
to stay, things to see, do, eat and buy

GW00702060

Benjamin Huie

with friends

UNTOURIST BRISBANE

Published by
UnTourist Co Pty Ltd
(A.C.N. 064 272 966)
PO Box 209
Balmain NSW 2041 Australia

Tel (02) 9974 1326; Fax 9974 1396
e-mail: info@untourist.com.au
www.untourist.com.au

Editorial director
Suzanne Baker

Design and production team
Benjamin Huie, Jacqueline Huie

Principal photography
Benjamin Huie

Printed by
David J. File Printers

Although the author and publisher have tried to make the information as accurate as possible, they accept no responsibility for any loss, injury or inconvenience sustained by any person using this book.

Other Untourist guide books:
Untourist Tasmania
UnTourist Sydney

First published
July, 1998
© Copyright UnTourist Co Pty Ltd 1998
ISBN 0-9585550-0-1

Underneath the arches of the Riverside Expressway – an alternative commuter route for roller-bladers, bike-riders and walkers.

So what is an untourist and am I one?

They could be 18-year-old-backpackers or 80-year-old "nomads". Being an untourist hasn't got much to do with age. You'll find them in most countries of the world. They are the kind of people who would trek through the wilderness carrying biscuits, cheese and wine-soaked maps rather than relax in the comfort of an air-conditioned tour bus. They would drive past four convenient motels with pool, air con, en suite and TV, in search of some quaint off-road "mum and dad" guesthouse with dubious plumbing – just because it offers home-baked bread and wide verandahs.

Are they like eco-tourists, green tourists, cultural tourists, alternative tourists and educational tourists? Yes, they would identify, to a greater or lesser degree, with all those labels. The thing that fuses these fellow-travellers together into a resolute band, however, is their shared dislike of touristy places. Some may prefer opera to bird-watching, or silk pillows to camping, but they will all seek out the "authentic" environments, both man-made and natural, avoiding those either spoiled by, or developed for, the tourist trade. Whether they find it in a backpacker hostel or a grand hotel, untourists seek simplicity rather than pretension, style rather than luxury, and value for money – regardless of cost.

THE AUTHORS:

BENJAMIN HUIE A popular Sydney arts photographer and, more recently, travel writer, Benjamin gathered an extensive local Brisbane research team. He became a part-time resident, took along his two pre-teen daughters Lucy and Nell, and drew on the resources of a complement of family connections and friends.

JAN POWER Born in Stanthorpe, Queensland, and educated in Brisbane, Jan is a well-known Brisbane personality with a particular expertise in food (she's a London Cordon Bleu graduate). Jan is a witty opinion giver via, radio, TV and print on all subjects, but especially the arts and food of Brisbane.

JACQUELINE HUIE A founder of UnTourist Co. Adjunct Professor of Tourism Studies, University of Queensland, Jacqueline has often been an outspoken critic of the big development trends of Australian tourism. Through the Joseph Banks Group, she researched, analysed and forecast the impact of tourism in Australia. She predicted the rise of independent travellers and their need for an appropriate information system – hence the formation of the UnTourist Co. Jacqueline wrote UnTourist Sydney.

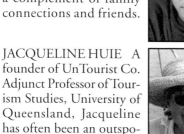

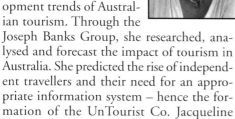

SUZANNE BAKER Editorial Director. After a career in journalism and film, including producing the 1976 Academy Award winning film Leisure, she wrote the book of and produced the internationally acclaimed documentary series, The Human Face of China. She also produced the mini series Land of Hope. Suzanne joined the Joseph Banks Group in 1988, became co-founder of the UnTourist Co and wrote UnTourist Tasmania.

Thanks to the savvy locals

Benjamin Huie would first like to thank the untourist home team, also Nell and Lucy Huie (what a pair); Kate Yeomans, Godfrey and the chooks for the eggs, John Huie snr, Beverley and Mullie, Anna and David Frogget – thanks for putting up everyone; the Stantons (sorry Ben burnt your saucepan); Cala, Melenie and Julian White (and all the gang at the Hotel Sorento); Aunty Margaret Iselin, Lafe Charlton, Jim Anderson, Peter Kelly, Ben Wilson and the BIQ; Eddie Liu, Peter Spinner, Tiga Bayles, Paul Ewart, Stephen Clark, Mark Paddenburg, Alan Warrie, Casey O'Hare, Cathy Goodwin, Olga Riha, Angelo Comero, Jane Hodges, Anne Louise McCrea, Karyn Merser, Bruce Hood, Rod Howard, Lisa Ferguson, Peter Sawyer, Bob and Ros Beeton, Barbara and Jim Graham, David Malouf, William Frazer, Dale Spender, Ross and Crisha Woods, Sadie Wilson, Philip Bacon, Jude Munro, Janet Campbell, The UnTourist Co wishes to recognise the support of the Queensland Tourist and Travel Corporation and the City of Sundays Marketing team, the Brisbane City Council, Brisbane Tourism and the John Oxley Library.

Photographic credits

The photographs on pages 51,53,56 and 143 were taken by Councillor David Hinchcliffe, from his book "Two to the Valley". The look and feel of these photographs is very untourist, thank you David, they look great.

The John Oxley library supplied the photographs on pages.....15, 20, 21, 29, 30, 34, 35, 38, 44, 48, 49, 71, 110, 111, 113, 126, 127, 128, 129, 134, 188, 190,198, 198 and 199. Pages 11, 12, 13, 189 and 192 Supplied by the QTTC. Page 14 supplied by Simon at Fire-Works. The map from 1888 on pages 16,17 and 196 was supplied by Heritage Editions. Page 30 and 97 (William Jolly bridge) from a shot supplied by Yellow Submarine. Page 72 supplied by UQP, page 84/5 Suzanne Baker, page 191 The UnTourist Co. Page 196 Bill Mansill; page 100 and 132 supplied by Outdoor Pursuits Group; page 101Alen Warrie,page 116 of Anna Yen by Reina Irmer page 117 (LaBoite) Melenie Gray. Page 118 supplied by Kooemba Jdarra, page 120 supplied by QAG, page 125 supplied by Jackie McKimmie, page135 photograph by Duane Hart supplied by Queensland Rugby Union Ltd. page 136 supplied by Queensland Cricket, page 134 supplied by Peter Kelly, QRU. The shots on page 159 were supplied by the subjects, page 160 ad 167 supplied by Herron Pharmaceuticals. All others by Benjamin Huie.

YOU CAN'T BUY YOUR WAY INTO AN UNTOURIST GUIDE BOOK
We take no advertising or payment of any kind. Recommendations that make it into Untourist guide books are earned by merit only. It's nice to know that there are some things money can't buy.

For telephone numbers and addresses, see the yellow pages Directory at the back

CONTENTS

"What is an untourist and am I one?" Being an untourist hasn't got much to do with age. You'll find them in most countries of the world. Are they like eco-tourists, green tourists, cultural tourists, alternative tourists and educational tourists? Yes, they would identify, to a greater or lesser degree, with all those labels.

Untourist guides are put together with insider information. Here is the list of key contributors.

Untourist Brisbane is a selective guide – the criteria for selection, the duck award system explained.

We choose the five best things about Brisbane: The Access; The Wild Things; The Figs and Bugs; The River Highway; The Quirkiness.

How "slatternly" Brisbane has turned from Queensland's ungainly city into the star turn in Australia's most diverse and exotic state. Now Australia's fastest growing city, Brisbane started out as a walled gaol. With its fast-flowing River highway, outdoor cafesand burgeoning cultural scene, and the feeling of ease about it – yes, Brisbane is looking great

In the 1830s, under the rule of the "Beast of Brisbane", Captain Patrick Logan, Brisbane was Australia's most feared convict settlement. By the time it had become dubbed "River City", Brisbane had the good life well and truly on offer: River transport, restaurants, historic sites and plenty of places for sitting, playing and dreaming.

The convict buildings – The Old Mill and the Commissariat Store; the Governor's black guard; the Logans and the Petries; the Battle of Brisbane; shopping and eating in the centre; the Botanic Gardens; the seats of government.

The Great Land Scam of 1848; Two to The Valley for the food and the pubs; Eddie's Chinatown; bikes and books at Newstead and New Farm; the old things of Paddington and the city within a city – the University of Queensland.

From dockland past to contemporary arts, home of Brisbane's most culturally diverse suburb, West End and to the seaside towns for nostalgia and fish and chips.

From the "I really can't afford it, but I want something wonderful" to: "I want something wonderful but I have to watch

(**6 Places to Stay** cont'd)
the budget and "I want something wonderful but at a rock bottom price". A grand hotel and little personal ones; serviced apartments, guesthouses and backpacker hostels.

The sort of things that make the savvy locals glad they live in Brisbane. Ranging from hanging off a cliff from a rope, to cheap ways to fill in a few hours when the weather's "crook". Brisbane has plenty of things to do, especially out-of-doors – and some fine indoors ones as well. Includes special experiences rather than one-offs.

Mrs Croft's obscene act; David Malouf - a writer's town; Matilda's portentous wink and nod; getting the most from the South Bank; Murri art and the Kooemba Jdarra theatre; the major Arts performers and the fringe theatres; Brisbane rock, jazz; the best galleries; film and cinemas.

How a sport had preference over training the troops preparing for war in the Pacific; legendary stories, cricket, football, golf, fishing and more

The best local produce and where to eat it; from stodge to style in 10 years; Brisbane's pioneer chefs and the very best restaurants, cafes and brasseries; the best pubs – both old and "born-again style"; Brisbane booze - both wine and beer; delis, and Ben's cheap eats.

Where to get the best local product, including Murri artefacts; how to find the bargains, markets, shopping and the antiques circuit.

Visitors' information; how the transport system works; information on buses, ferries, parking, shuttle services; emergency services and advice.

The pick of day trips out of Brisbane, the locals favourite short breaks including the Sunshine Coast, the off-shore islands, the Darling Downs and the hinterlands.

Your handy reference for addresses and telephone numbers of places and special features mentioned in the guide.

About our other publications and special information services.

A Guide to the Guide

Untourist Brisbane is a selective guide-book. To be more explicit, we have selected and recommended only things that meet our criteria. If you happen to share our philosophy about what makes a great place to stay, or what constitutes a terrific meal, then you will get a great deal of useful information out of this guidebook. On the other hand, if you are of a different persuasion, you could end up complaining that we left out a lot of perfectly good motels or tours...and we are probably guilty as charged.

All about Ducks

Our symbol of excellence derives from that previously common trio of glossy coloured pottery ducks that invariably adorned the wall-papered lounge of every suburban bungalow in Australia during the '50s. Long may they fly. We chose these ducks as our symbol of excellence as a reminder that architecture, design, the arts, food and wine have, indeed, taken a giant flight forward.

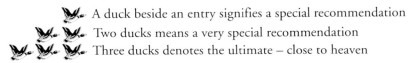

A duck beside an entry signifies a special recommendation

Two ducks means a very special recommendation

Three ducks denotes the ultimate – close to heaven

Dollar symbols and what they mean

When it comes to cost, we believe all our recommendations to be good value for money regardless of their prices.

Addresses and telephone numbers

For easy sourcing of our recommendations throughout the guide, use our handy directory of telephone numbers and addresses at the start of the yellow pages at the back.

The disabled

Facilities for the disabled are extensive in Brisbane – eg kerbs of most key footpaths provide easy wheelchair access and the vast majority of accommodation places have appropriate facilities.

Free updates

Information becomes out-of-date, new places emerge, and recommendations need to be regularly amended. Updated and changed information is entered on our web site weekly, (to receive by mail, see page 211). You will also find links to other sites that can give you current events information. Log on to: **www.untourist.com.au**

Criteria for selection

The final recommendations in this book are based on the following criteria:
• They are not predominantly patronised by mass-market tourists or, if they are, it is because they are in a class by themselves, eg, Taj Mahal or Buckingham Palace.
• They do not impose themselves, but are part of the local environment.
• They are patronised by discerning locals and appeared on their "favourite" lists.
• They meet the UnTourist Co's standards of excellence, checked out by our recseachers.
• A decade of market research conducted by the Joseph Banks Group (our founding company) into the likes and dislikes of the independent traveller, judged them to be what our particular reader is seeking.

The Best Things About Brisbane

THE ACCESS Nowhere can you get such easy access to so many tourist and – more important – untourist places in Australia (see 13 OUT OF BRISBANE). But as yet, the only people who seem to be aware of this are those who live in Brisbane.

WILD THINGS OF BRISBANE You can hear the crows in George Street – this is a fair dinkum bush city. The Brisbane City Council (BCC) even provides information on how to encourage wildlife in suburban backyards.

THE RIVER HIGHWAY The Brisbane River and its fledgling transport system is certainly one of the best things about Brisbane – in fact it is hard to imagine the metamorphosis of Brisbane taking place without the River's rediscovery. A glance at the changes that have evolved on its banks over the last 10 years clearly indicates where Brisbane's future lies. (2 THE RIVER)

FIGS AND BUGS Moreton Bay bugs drizzled over with lemon and melted butter. Yum. Just sit under Moreton Bay figs, don't eat them. They hang on hand-some, giant, fairytale trees with trunks and roots systems that hold the ground like elephant legs.

THE QUIRKINESS It's an Australian thing, a bush thing, and very much a Queensland thing. It's being different, anti-authority – maybe it's Irish in origin. You see it in the odd characters in The Valley, the twist and flourish of the entrepreneurs and the defiant politics. If you're close to it, you probably don't see it, but when you move away and revisit, then you recognise it. You can't send it home on a postcard but this non-conformist Australian quirkiness is still a precious part of Brisbane. In time, as the city becomes more international, it will be lost, so seek it out while you still can.

NOTE: Brisbane is one of the "Best Things About Queensland" in the book *Untourist Queensland*

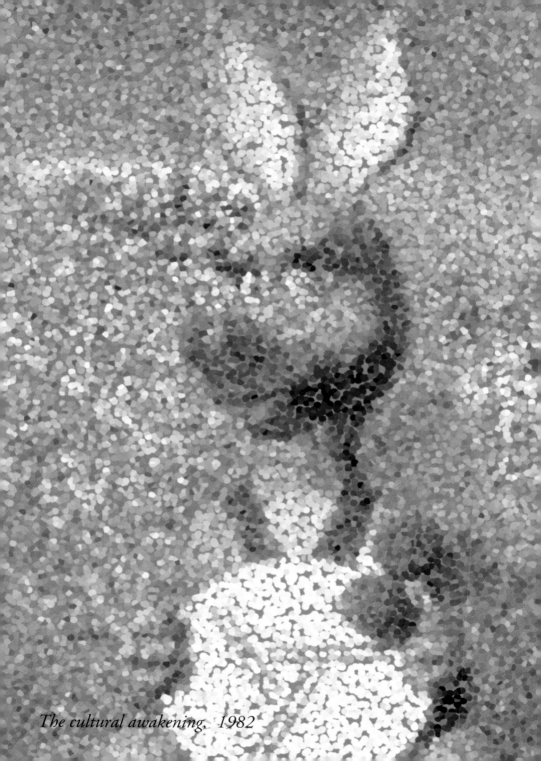

The cultural awakening, 1982

1 Brisbane ✔

Tourists (unlike *un*tourists) tend to be rather acquisitive with their leisure time. Holidays mean ticking off the icons. Been there, done that. The Gold Coast ✔ the Big Pineapple ✔ Fiji ✔. No icons, no visits and Brisbane is certainly not a place with renowned icons – no Buckingham Palace, no Statue of Liberty here. So far as the tourist groups are concerned, it has been more a place you pass through on the way to the Gold Coast an hour's drive to the south, or the Sunshine Coast an hour and a half's drive to the north, or a place to fly over as you head for Queensland's Far North – Cairns ✔ or the Great Barrier Reef ✔. And 20 years ago, there was some justification in not putting Brisbane on your visit list. Here is what celebrated writer and Brisbane National Treasure, David Malouf's volatile character in *Johnno* said about Brisbane in the 1950's:

"Brisbane is so sleepy, so slatternly, so sprawlingly unlovely. I have taken to wandering about after school looking for one simple object in that it might be romantic, or appealing even, but there is nothing. It is simply the most ordinary place in the world."

After achieving some notoriety during World War II as the first capital city in Australia's line of defence from Japanese invasion ("The Brisbane Line"), Brisbane then went into a bit of a post-war slump and stayed there for about 30 years. Lots of action was happening in the vastness of Queensland, but it all seemed to be happening in some place other than Brisbane – minerals, beef and wool were booming in the west; pineapples, bananas,

c. 1950 Where's Brisbane ?

peanuts, tobacco in the north; sugarcane farms were sprinkled liberally up and down the coast and tourism was building in the neighbouring Gold Coast area.

Because of the immense size and diversification of Queensland, more convenient ports and outlets were developed rather than the trade funnelling through the capital city, inconveniently tucked down in the south-eastern corner of the state. The world seemed to be by–passing Brisbane.

It was not until the '80s, when Brisbane was chosen as the site of the 1982 Commonwealth Games, that the city started to take on some shine. It is common local knowledge that the catalyst for this cultural awakening was a 13 metre fibreglass kangaroo. Tottering above the adoring crowd during the pomp and splendour of the Games' victory procession, the very official, slightly cross-eyed mascot with its three mechanical parts, turned its head and winked. The crowd roared and the word was about that:

"When that old 'roo turned his head and winked, Brissie just up and took off".

THE INCREDIBLE MOVING PARTS OF MATILDA

EYE WINKS

HEAD NODS AND TURNS

PRIVATE PARTS REPLACED BY POUCH TRAPDOOR REVEALING 100 KIDDIES IN JOEY SUITS

The cultural awakening – detail.

But the lights really twinkled when our very own Brissie was selected as the site for the World Expo of 1988. In preparation, the Brisbane City Council launched its River '88 Strategy with the slogan – "Brisbane, the River City" and an old wharf on the southern bank became the focus for the Bicentennial World Fair. This dilapidated structure was regarded as an unfitting neighbour for the splendid Cultural Centre taking shape at both sides of the southern end of the Victoria Bridge. So it became part of the site and a million or two flocked to the riverside Expo '88, bringing renewed attention to the concept of water-borne commuter transport, and a greater appreciation of the riverside outdoor cafe lifestyle that marked the birth of socialising on a large scale.

Rising from Expo, the South Bank complex is now a continuous festival of living theatre, street markets, eateries, buskers, pubs, with the varied and best butterfly collection in the southern hemisphere. Brisbane has been revitalised culturally, socially and economically. So maybe it was the wink and nod from that old kangaroo that did the trick. The international events, and the stream of people and money that followed, kicked off a whole lot of potential that had been dormant for years. New places to eat, arts and entertainment events sprang up and the Brisbane Broncos won more games than ever. The people of Brisbane seemed to discover that they not only had a great place to live but also a city they wanted to show off to the world.

Under one roof

To get this surprisingly large city into some sort of perspective, particularly for those who are visitors to the country, Brisbane is the third largest single municipality in the world after Los Angeles and New York. The key here is the word "municipality". Unlike most cities, which are broken up into many small local government precincts, Brisbane is under one roof, so to speak – under the authority of the Brisbane City Council. Many feel that this is a great advantage as it has helped to galvanise its direction and sense of purpose in everything that is done, from getting all the loos to flush with a new sewage system, to building an arts complex and getting the water transport service up and happening – all in record time.

There are more Aboriginal people in Queensland than any other state in Australia, and in Brisbane they appear to have a relatively high level of involvement in local government. The **Campfire boardroom** shown below should not, however, be taken as a typical example. It was taken at the 1996 Asia Pacific Triennial, held at the Queensland Art Gallery. For those who are particularly interested in Aboriginal tours, art, theatre and history, there are many references and entries throughout this book in the appropriate chapters.

The term **Murri** is often used in the text and is the favoured local word to describe the Aboriginal people of Queensland and northern New South Wales. It is another less generalised name for Australia's original inhabitants. It means simply 'our people'. The word **Koori** (or **Koorie**) has the same meaning when applied to the eastern states of Australia. In the Northern Territory the preferred word is **Yolngu**; **Nyunga** in Western Australia; **Aranda** in central Australia; and **Nungga** in South Australia.

On being different

Brisbane is the founding city and the seat of government for Australia's feisty, " twice-as-big-as-Texas", frontier state. If you scratch the city's new-found patina of gentrification, you'll find some of the defiant individualism that has characterised Queenslanders and led them to being seen by other Australians – and indeed by themselves – as being "different". They accept, with a certain pride, that they have always been out of step with their southern neighbours politically, socially, even chronologically. In every eastern state in Australia, folks put their clocks on or back to get more useable daylight time – except Queensland. This can be very confusing for visitors and locals alike as planes, trains and buses are sometimes missed. So visitors be warned, check your Queensland times.

Capital under threat

A glance at a map of Queensland shows the capital tucked away in the lower south-east corner, traitorishly close to the New South Wales border. To drive from Cooktown in Far North Queensland (abbreviated by the irreverent to Effin' Q) to Brisbane is around 2000 km. These vast distances between the other towns in Queensland and its capital have been the cause of the thrust and parrying from the Far North in its quest for secession from the state. Brisbane, they reckon, is too far away and only looks after the interests of the "southerners". In fact, Brisbane has been close to losing the role of Queensland capital on many occasions. Currently the push from the Far North is for Cairns to be its capital – tomorrow it might be Townsville. They have Buckley's chance, of course, but those northerners keep up the pressure with cries of "southerners don't understand us". Interestingly enough, this is exactly the same cry that Queensland has used on its "southerner" states New South Wales, Victoria and the federal capital, Canberra, in the argument for Queensland secession from Australia...ho hum.

Sir Thomas Brisbane, the under achiever

Did he fall, or was he pushed?

Brisbane was named after the high-born well-educated and lucratively married Sir Thomas Makdougall Brisbane who, after an illustrious military career in Ireland, Flanders, the West Indies and America, and after being praised by Wellington, knighted by the King and applauded by the British Parliament, made the terrible mistake in 1824 of applying for the job of Governor of New South Wales (when New South Wales was the name of the entire colony rather than just one state as it is today). Poor Sir Thomas was recalled to London before his term was up and went down in history as one of Australia's great under achievers – with a little help from self-seeking colonials such as arch capitalist John Macarthur, the very Reverend and very machiavellian Samuel Marsden, who took every opportunity to put both boot and knife into the new governor. Unlike his predecessor, Governor Lachlan Macquarie, who was a frenetic builder/developer, Governor Brisbane made a further terrible career move by concentrating his efforts on the legitimising of land titles in the new colony, thus managing to get up everyone's nose. As a number of contemporary Australian political leaders have discovered to their chagrin, trying to sort out the legitimacy of titles and land claims – take Wik and Mabo, for example – can be a thankless task. And Brisbane himself should have known better as he had described the real estate scene in the colony in 1821 as: *"Not a cow calves in the colony but her owner applies for an additional grant in consequence of the increase of his stock".*

No doubt, he meant well. Wellington commented on Brisbane's recall to Britain: *"There are many brave men not fit to be Governors of colonies."*

Brisbane's dubious beginnings as a walled gaol, then being named after a real loser and now under threat from the north for being hidden away in the southern corner of its own state – none of this has held it back one bit. In fact, old Brissie is turning out to be a bit of a star. It is the fastest growing capital city in the country. Smart Australians are moving to Brisbane to avoid the crushing costs of cities such as Sydney and Melbourne. At a time of internationalisation, when many Australians question the loss of their traditional characteristics, Brisbane, the most quintessential "Australian" Australian city, is looking very attractive. It seems to fulfil the stereotype at a time when we all seem to be seeking a return to some back-to-basics values, an easier life, a clean place in the sun. With its warmth, its streets lined by palms and shaded by giant old fig trees, its gardens of tropical frangipani and bougainvillea, its fast-flowing River highway, outdoor cafes and burgeoning cultural scene, and the feeling of ease about it – yes, Brisbane is looking great.

Coat of arms.

Brisbane River 1880 – supplied by Heritage Editions,
see 11 BEST THINGS TO BUY

2 The River

INCLUDES: The old brown belt; The Beast of Brisbane; the racist River; a beach on the River; about the ferries; about the Bridges; places to see from the River.

From the air, the Brisbane River could be an old brown belt with the buckle in Mount Stanley and the tail in Moreton Bay. It's a bit like Main Street in most country towns. Everything settles around it and we all know where it is closest to our homes. It links and binds the city together. Like most Main Streets, it has its good bits and its crook bits. The crook bits are around the tail of the belt. At the entrance you see a flat, partly industrialised airport landscape; at the buckle end, where the River begins, deer still stoop to drink from puddles at Mount Stanley and a single prawn catcher is allowed to cast his net at the River's mouth as Italian fishermen did at night 80 years ago using kerosene lamps.

Wharf remnants at Gardens Point.

The Brisbane River is about the length and general shape of London's Thames, but not quite as decoratively fringed, built-over, or tunnelled under as yet. Busy and bustling River furniture comprises such multicultural surprises as Yankee paddle steamers, foreign yachts, a vast old car ferry that has been themed into an excessively lit permanent party island for hire, Venetian gondolas, a Chinese junk, many high-powered catamaran ferries the CityCats, old tugboats decorated with car tyres, open ferries and recreational boats of every type, from high-powered motor boats to metal dinghies and kayaks. A more graceful sight in the early morning is of athletes and competitive school boys and girls, skimming along in racing sculls past fishermen's prawn trawlers.

The River has seen many changes since European settlers wet their feet here 170 years ago but they're mere ripples compared to today's flood of fun, food, festivals and frivolity going on around this busy and exciting waterway. After ignoring it for years, everybody now wants a river view: builders and developers are reinventing Brisbane as a river city with high corporate and residential tower-dwellers paying heaps to watch the water activity from their balconies high above its long, winding trail. City workers are even snubbing the bridges and river expressway that snakes along the south-east bank and taking to the River in great numbers in the flotilla of watercraft on offer.

After being viewed for years largely from garages and outdoor dunnies (because everything was built to look the other way), Brisbane has now turned itself around to face its handsome River and, for the second time in its short history, the Brisbane River has been discovered.

First cat on the River

"Trim" accompanied Matthew Flinders on board the HMS Norfolk when he navigated Moreton Bay in 1799. Around that time, the famous navigator wrote to his sailing mate, surgeon George Bass, suggesting that sailors on long voyages should be able to bring along their wives. For without such company the extreme loneliness would encourage friendship with "cabin boys" or "cats". Hmm.

THE SOURCE OF THE RIVER

The whole area at the mouth of the River was first noted and named *Morton* Bay, by Captain Cook in 1770. In 1773, this event was recorded and then misspelled Moreton Bay by Cook's biographer John Hawksworth in his 1773 Cook book: *An account of a voyage round the World by Lieutenant James Cook.* The area was then seriously explored, mapped and misspelled once more in 1799 by the brilliant navigator Lieut Matthew Flinders.

A Garden of Eden

It was not for another 20 years, in 1823, that the actual River was explored. John Oxley Esq, Surveyor General of New South Wales explored the River in his cutter Mermaid, and named it to honor Sir Thomas Brisbane, the then Governor of New South Wales. Mind you, had the homesick Scot, Chief Justice Sir Frances Forbes had his way, it was going to be named Edinglassie after his home in Scotland. Another report credits this suggestion as coming from Brisbane's first free settler, Andrew Petrie, who, when he first saw the River was purported to have called it Eden Glassy, a different spelling, because its "rising mists and glassy calm reminded [him] of a garden of Eden in the lush Brisbane valley" well, maybe you had to be there at the time...Next in the "name the area" contest came the local Murries' Oompie Bong, meaning deserted or dead dwelling places. Later, with no improvement in sight, this was corrupted into Humpybong. Mercifully, these two were both changed to what is now Redcliffe Peninsula, north of the River.

North from Brisbane to Sydney

With quite a reputation as an explorer to live up to and convinced he was the first European to set foot on the River bank, the ambitious Oxley (pictured) must have been pretty miffed to round the bend and see a couple of perfectly naked white fellers fishing on the banks.

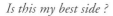

The story goes: Four ex-convicts, Pamphlet, Finnegan, Thomson and their mate Parsons, had been set a task to sail south of the new colony of Port Jackson (Sydney) in search of millable timber. Though they were regarded as experienced sailors, they inexplicably left Sydney Cove without a navigational device. As a consequence of this oversight, the three convicts (Thomson had fallen overboard during a storm) found themselves, not south of Port Jackson, but north – about a 1000 miles north in fact, on the low sandy shore of Moreton Island near Brisbane. Adopted by members of the local Aboriginal tribe, and believing they were still south of Sydney, Finnegan and Parsons left Pamphlet and set out to travel north to get back to Sydney.

Is this my best side ?

Disappointed and no doubt confused, Finnegan split with Parsons and returned to join

Pamphlet. It was these two who were fishing with the tribe on the banks of the River when John Oxley sailed up the bay. Oxley returned to Sydney with the two feral convicts and delivered a rave report on the River and the general area. Later, in 1824 when he returned with a detachment of the 40th Regiment and a party of convicts to claim these virgin, uncharted shores, he rounded the bend and discovered yet another white feller – this time it was Parsons, the last remaining convict of the original four. He had also failed to find Sydney by travelling north and had managed to struggle back to the local tribe in time to greet Oxley's party. History does not record Oxley's comments. This time Oxley sailed 50 miles up the River, as far as what is now called the Ipswich area, and sent back another, even more approving report to Governor Brisbane on the fine waterway and its surrounding arable soil. At the time, however, the Governor didn't have agriculture or free settlers on his mind for the new riverlands. Rather, he saw the Moreton Bay with its fine Brisbane River as solving a more pressing and sinister problem.

The Beast of Brisbane

In 1822 the government of mad King George III was pouring convicts into Sydney and Hobart with embarrassing zeal, and the administration of New South Wales was casting about for a new settlement that would serve to house the convict overflow. "...for the worst class of offenders." It was to Moreton Bay that the troublemakers, the ones who were too tough to handle in the south, were transported, and it was to become the most feared place in the young colony. At first they were based at the mouth of Moreton Bay; later, they were sent up the River to a walled gaol that would be renamed Brisbane. For these unfortunates this place was a hell on earth, a hell that inspired one of the most plaintive and enduring songs to come from Australia's convict past.

Logan – dressed to kill.

Moreton Bay

One Sunday morning, as I went walking,
by Brisbane waters I chanced to stray;
I heard a convict his fate bewailing,
as on the sunny river bank I lay:
"I am a native of Erin's Island,
but banished now from my native shore.
They stole me from my aged parents,
and from the maiden whom I adore.

I've been a prisoner at Port Macquarie,
at Norfolk Island and Emu Plains,
at Castle Hill and at cursed Toongabbie,
at all these settlements I've been in chains;
But of all the places of condemnation
and penal stations in New South Wales,
to Moreton Bay I have found no equal,
excessive tyranny each day prevails.

For three long years I was beastly treated,
and heavy irons on my legs I wore,
my back with flogging was lacerated,
and oft times painted with my crimson gore.
And many a man from downright starvation
lies mouldering now underneath the clay;
and Captain Logan he had us mangled
all on the triangles of Moreton Bay.

Like the Egyptians and ancient Hebrews,
we were oppressed under Logan's yolk
'til a native black lying there in ambush
did deal this tyrant his mortal stroke.
My fellow prisoners be exhilarated
that all such monsters like death may find,
and when from bondage we are liberated
our former sufferings will fade from mind.

This folk song assured eternal infamy for Captain Patrick Logan – the Beast of Brisbane, soldier and dictator of the little walled goal by the River where no free man was allowed to trespass within 50 miles of its boundaries. Logan took command of the new colony in 1826 and was given absolute authority over both convicts and the growing number of surrounding settlers by Governor Brisbane who, at this time, didn't really have his mind on the job because he was in the process of being given the boot and sent back to from whence he came.

Not being burdened by notions of compassion or conscience, and having the newly appointed Governor Darling also turning a blind eye to his methods, Logan literally worked the chained convicts to death as he flogged and bullied the town into some sort of shape.

The current settlement and south reaches of the River formed a moat around the gaol. Later when the town was opened to free settlers, the River was used as an artificial barrier to separate the feared Aboriginal tribes – "the cannibal savages"– from the respectable church-going white citizens.

River Doings

This north and south River segregation went on in a less official but just as effective form, until the late 1940s. During World War II, when Brisbane was seen to be under threat of Japanese invasion and the US had sent their forces to help in its defence, the River played an even more blatantly racist role, separating the black American servicemen from their white GI comrades. At the time, the White Australia Policy (or, to give it its official name, the Immigration Restriction Act) was entrenched in national policy. The Act, introduced in 1902 and still in force until 1973, was implemented to protect the jobs of the good (white) Aussie workers from the bad (non-white) Polynesians and Chinese immigrants who, as workers, were better value for money and therefore seen as a national threat.

City of the Future

In less than 150 years, from its sordid beginnings as a walled convict community, the city of Brisbane has emerged as an Australian city of the future. It is blessed with a sunny climate, the most wonderful and accessible surroundings, and traced by a fine river that curls around it to line and enhance its many modern attractions.

Putting on a good face to the River

Brisbane's smart, swift catamarans (**CityCats**) and 11 River ferries provide one of the best ways to view the cityscape and historical backwaters. They cost only a few dollars and will take you everywhere. A CityCat in local language is a high-speed million-dollar catamaran ferry seating 138 and is the most scenic, refreshing and often the fastest way to get around the city.

Because like most major river cities in the world Brisbane was built up around the River, the Cats cut through almost all the interesting areas. The Brisbane City Council's fleet of six operate from Bulimba, Breakfast Creek, Fortitude Valley, New Farm, and Gardens Point. Travelling at around 27 knots, they're equipped with mobile public phones, toilets, baby-change facilities and drinking fountains. Highly recommended as the best ride in town – particularly in the hot summer months.

Following a 19 kilometre watery route, you can see all the sights in more comfort than a cool carton of cucumbers. At the southern end, visit the **University of Queensland** – it has one of the best cinemas in town, live theatre and music (check newspapers), a beautiful campus with jacaranda trees, historic sandstone buildings (see 7 THINGS TO DO). Then on to **North Quay** (Brisbane city stop-off), across to South Bank and **Queensland Performing Arts Complex, Brisbane Convention and Exhibition Centre, South Bank Markets and old Conservatorium.**

Next stop, **Riverside Centre.** On Sunday 8am-3pm there are the **Riverside Markets** (see more below) a nationally recognised market, good for many hours of browsing and buying, alongside the Riverside Centre's extensive range of eateries.

And the Story is he didn't get a penny for his trouble (see page 30)

The Customs House

To take a gentle stroll along the riverside from Eagle Street Pier and end up at the Customs House for lunch would normally take about 10 minutes during the week but about two hours on the weekends – not because there are lots of people, but because when the market stalls are all lined up along the River, bulging with every offering from funny hats to falafels – there are many temptations along the way. **The Customs House Brasserie** tends to be more locally patronised – or at least it seems like that. Probably because the building is not a new phenomenon but very much part of Brisbane's riverside history.

Doing lunch by the River.

Marketing Mozart.

Riverside Markets

These excellent markets wind around three levels of the **Riverside Centre.** City-style eateries are within the building and you can find lots of snacks in the stalls, but nothing especially remarkable. It can get crowded, but a good market needs a crowd to keep it alive. (Sometimes you get the feeling of *déjà vu,* – weren't those the faces you saw at the other markets you checked out earlier?) This is the market where you'll find a lot of new gear, some beautiful clothes and furniture. The setting takes it up a few notches from the standard market scene Sunday: 8am–3pm. (See 11 BEST THINGS TO BUY).

New Farm Park

New Farm Park has a ferry stop and this is a great picnic spot (the park is famous for its roses). Gates open for vehicle access at 5am and close Mon-Thurs at 7pm; Fri-Sun at 9pm; pedestrian access, 24 hours. Its flat loop is good for bicycling and has plenty of shade – jaca-randas and fig trees abound. There are lovely rose beds and avenues with creepers, open space and nooks. Stop to re-fresh at the elegant **Tea Rooms** and there is a great playing area for the kids with fig tree roots cleverly incorporated in the playing equipment.

RIVER DOINGS

City

Riverside Markets – A nationally recognised market, good for many hours of browsing and buying, alongside the Riverside Centre's extensive range of eateries. **Customs House** – Take a gentle stroll along the riverside from Eagle Street Pier and end up at the Customs House for lunch. The Customs House is very much part of Brisbane's riverside history. **Breakfast stop** – Right on the Edward Street ferry stop is the Heritage, one of the finest hotels in the country. It's partly the easterly aspect that makes this charming, sunny, open-air place by the River a great al fresco breakfast spot. **Botanic Gardens** – beside the River and marking the spot of the settlement's first vegie patch, it is also the site of the elaborately festooned landing pontoon set up to greet the new Governor of Queensland in 1859.

University of Queensland This is not just a university, it's rather like a town within a city – theatres, cinemas, museums, sportsgrounds, cafes and one of the best bookshops in Brisbane.

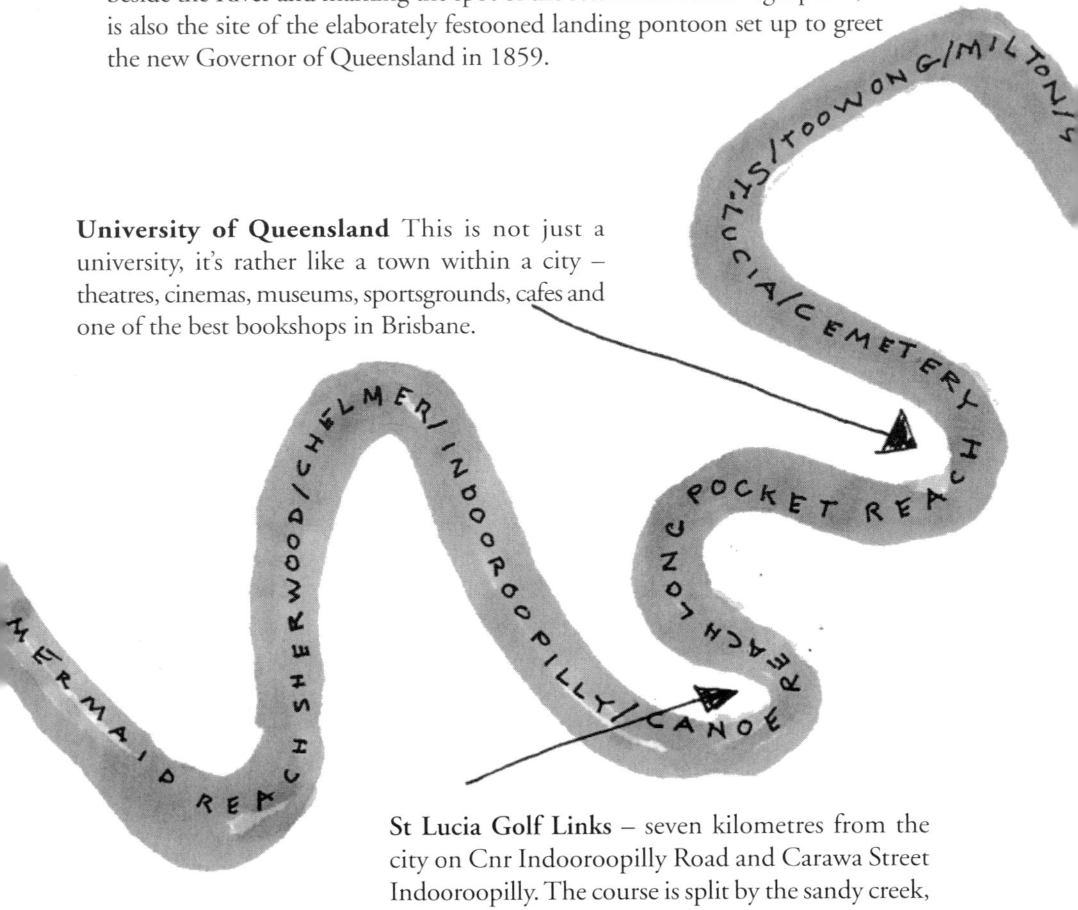

St Lucia Golf Links – seven kilometres from the city on Cnr Indooroopilly Road and Carawa Street Indooroopilly. The course is split by the sandy creek, and any water running though a golf course adds to its beauty and its difficulty factor.

ST LUCIA/TOOWONG/MILTON'S
LUCIA/CEMETERY
POCKET REACH
LONG REACH
CHELMER/INDOOROOPILLY/CANOE
SHERWOOD
MERMAID REACH

© UnTourist Co (1998)

Fishing Of course it's prohibited to fish off the Brisbane River bridges, but you can throw a line in at Newstead Park or the east side of the Captain John Bourke Park under the Story Bridge. We found an older woman who spoke very little English. She was using a hand line on the Brisbane River, at the Hamilton reach and already had a bucket full of flathead. She got across that she tried to come every day but her husband wouldn't.

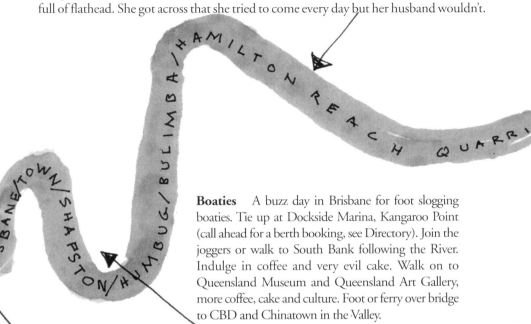

Boaties A buzz day in Brisbane for foot slogging boaties. Tie up at Dockside Marina, Kangaroo Point (call ahead for a berth booking, see Directory). Join the joggers or walk to South Bank following the River. Indulge in coffee and very evil cake. Walk on to Queensland Museum and Queensland Art Gallery, more coffee, cake and culture. Foot or ferry over bridge to CBD and Chinatown in the Valley.

South Bank The Parklands are a very well-crafted, well-landscaped inner city escape. Immediately post Expo '88 this place was a dust bowl. City Beach, is now one of the main area's of the South Bank Parklands. It has white sands and filtered water and is sealed off from the River. Featuring white regularly raked sands, clean clear filtered water. Sit (even better, float) and watch the River traffic go by and all only 10 minutes from work.

New Farm The prime riverfront address and often judged Brisbane's most livable suburb with easy access to the city by ferry, bus or bike. Traditional housing culture, multi-million-dollar development, a cosmopolitan mix of people and lively cafe culture have made it the darling of the urban renewal push. On the horizon ... redevelopment of the historic New Farm Powerhouse, destined to become a major cultural drawcard.

South Bank

Cross the River by ferry, CityCat, or you could walk across **Victoria Bridge** (sometimes the quickest way from town) to South Bank Parklands which, in addition to the markets, has **City Beach** (sealed off from the River) featuring white regularly raked sands, clean clear filtered water and lots of happy children. Pandanus tree groves overlook the beach and seem to have been there since the Jurassic Period. School holidays can be trouble but even then an early morning dip can lead you to daydreams of some major tropical retreat. Sit (even better, float) and watch the River traffic go by and all only 10 minutes from work. The South Bank arts precinct is another attraction here with the **Queensland Art Gallery, Conservatorium of Music, State Library of Queensland, Performing Arts Complex, and Queensland Museum** all jammed into a virtual cultural supermarket. There are more arts organisations in the surrounding area. (8 THE ARTS).

Bridges

The Walter Taylor Bridge. In 1924, Walter Taylor, a resident of Graceville (south side of the river at Indooroopilly), set up a progress association with the aim of promoting the idea of a crossing to link Graceville with Indooroopilly. Taylor's company, Indooroopilly Toll Bridge Ltd, eventually built the bridge. When the foundations were being set, gold was discovered in ore mixed with the concrete, but it was too late to remove the gold and there it still resides. The company did a canny deal with Doorman Long and Co to use the construction cable used to build the Sydney Harbour Bridge, which helped to keep the bridge within budget.

I grant you, Dr Bradfield, it is a well-contructed hat.

Story Bridge

The bridge's designer was Dr J. J. C. Bradfield who also designed Sydney Harbour Bridge. Born in nearby Sandgate, Bradfield was so passionate about his Story Bridge that he published several books including: *The story of the King George Memorial Bridge...From romance to Reality.* In spite of the grandiose title, he was an inspired designer.

His notions of materials coming from the local area and the almost lamplike structure of the bridge's profile shows us what made him the most popular bridge designer of his time. To be a worker on the bridge during the Great Depression was a great honour. After the bridge reached a certain height, the blokes were limited to one beer at smoko. When completed, the bridge was named after the humble John Douglas Story, who served as the vice-chancellor of the University of Queensland for 22 years without one cent of remuneration.

William Jolly Bridge

During the construction of the concrete and steel bridge, inflation was running high, costs were blowing out twofold and in 1931, there was a huge flood.

Story – no, not a penny.

William Jolly Bridge

The Story lingers on.

William Jolly, who was responsible for having the bridge built and called Grey Bridge, not only weathered the criticism but was re-elected as mayor. Eventually the bridge was named after him.

All of the more modern bridge work came in the Clem Jones era (Lord Mayor between 1961–75). One that had its effectiveness curtailed with the closure of Queen Street as a Mall was the **Victoria Bridge**, but is used by vehicles for easy access to the south.

BACK TO THE SOURCE

The first black settlers who drifted down from the Indonesian archipelago sometime between 100 and 40 thousand years ago (the anthropological jury is still out on this one) were content to fish and hunt calmly by the banks of this fast-flowing river. Building development and acquisitive progress were not core values in their belief system. They had different ways.

When the first white "invaders" came, the River lost its spiritual significance and took on a purely functional role – transport, waste disposal and, for many decades, it became a moat separating people of different skin colour and social standing.

New Farm Park, The Gabba in the background.

In the hands of the current custodians of the River, the 21st-century citizens of Brisbane – entrepreneurs, dedicated to growth, progress, and the good life – the River fares much better. It has returned to its rightful place as a central contributor to the lifestyle of its settlement, which is now the handsome, fast-growing, multicultural city of Brisbane.

In World War II, bomb shelters were built in Elizabeth Street

3 Centre

INCLUDES: *The convict buildings – The Old Mill and the Commissariat Store; the Governor's black guard; the Logans and the Petries; the Battle of Brisbane; shopping and eating in the centre; the Botanic Gardens; the seats of government*

Queensland has a number of towns and cities that appear to be in transition, either because they were something once and now the world has passed them by (like the mining towns of Palmerston and Herberton); or because they have become tourist places like Cairns and Surfers Paradise; or because they seem to be mindlessly growing without purpose, like Coomera or Smithfield.

Brisbane, however, is a proper city – as befits the capital of Queensland, the great Australian frontier state. And the centre of the city – which is where Brisbane began, and hence, where Queensland began – is a proper city centre, housing the major shopping and general business interests as well as the various seats of government power.

The only surviving convict structures in Brisbane, both built under the tyrannic Beast of Brisbane, Capt Patrick Logan. The Old Mill (left page), once erroneously called the Government Observatory, stands on the corner of Wickham Terrace and Bartlett Street without its windmill blades or original dome-like roof. Though called The Observatory, it never actually served this function – unless one uses the term broadly as in "to observe". In fact, it never functioned too well as anything particularly useful – unless you feel that dropping a metal ball from the dome at one o'clock each day or hanging convicted felons from the windmill's sails usefully served the residents. It is uncertain whether the pick-axe murderer of the Commissariat Store (1828) was hung from the windmill but the story goes that during the building of this store to house the early colony's produce, convict John Brungar took to a co-worker with a pick-axe. Two years later, Logan himself was beaten to death with what were assumed to be, nulla-nullas (Murri hunting weapons). The Commissariat Store is now the site of a fine Museum and the Royal Historical Society of Queensland , where you can get a clear idea of the trappings and conditions of those painful early days . The Commissariat Store, 115 William Street is open Tuesday to Friday from 11am–2pm and Sunday from 11am –4pm.

The Old Mill was built as a windmill to grind maize for food, which it did ineffectively. Not that this daunted the dreaded Captain Logan, who would set his wretched half-starved work gangs to operate the treadmill, the "never ending staircase", as a particularly sadistic punishment. As that was its prime purpose, it was immaterial whether the mill ground grain or not, and mostly it did not. Service calls were hard to come by in those days, and the rest of the convict construction in Brisbane at the time was of poor quality. Finally, in 1837, Andrew Petrie, an experienced builder, was summoned to fix the mill. He was allowed to live within the walled city, thus becoming Brisbane's first free citizen. Over the years he bred a whole bunch of useful Petries who were to become a most prominent Brisbane dynasty. You can find a mayor and quite a few Petrie streets, closes and terraces in Brisbane but, astonishingly, you will find nearly as many named after Logan.

Purported to be a convict drawing showing the windmill intact.

While on the subject of Brisbane streets. It is interesting to note that all the women's names **Ann, Adelaide, Queen, Mary,** *etc go east to west, while all the men's names,* **George, Albert, Edward** *run north to south. We do not believe this is a gender-specific statement....come to think of it, it is actually quite useful.*

'DANGEROUS SAVAGES' – GUARD OF HONOUR

After the convict settlement was closed in 1839, free settlers pushed hard for separation from New South Wales. Their wish was graciously granted by Queen Victoria in 1858 and, from its brand-new capital Brisbane, Queensland became a separate state. But there was a nasty surprise when it was realised that the new state had little or no real autonomy or money. This was the result of the NSW government doing some deft asset stripping in the lead-up to the event and the new colony was left without even enough soldiers to form an honour guard for the new Governor. Showing true Queensland resourcefulness, the citizens of Brisbane, aided by one of those Petries (Robert), who was on good terms with the local Murries, cobbled together a motley group. Dolled up splendidly in uniforms and decorations, they stood with muscats shouldered, forming a most colourful guard of honour for His Excellency. The curious thing was that no one seemed to notice that the new Governor was flanked by a guard of armed "dangerous savages". Considering the attitude held at the time by the citizens of Brisbane toward the Murries, perhaps the Welcome Committee used the "tamed" Murries as a reassuring show of control for the Governor.

The building from which the new Governor of Queensland made his announcement of separation, **Adelaide House**, still stands. That's the good news. The bad news is that you can't get inside to see it because it is now the home of the dean of **St John's Cathedral** in the church grounds between Ann and Adelaide Streets. You can certainly call in at the entrance in Ann Street, however, and speak to the people if you want to see the building from the outside.

His Excellency Sir George Ferguson Bowen, Knight Commander of the Most Distinguished Order of St Michael and St George, Captain-General and Governor-in-Chief of the Colony of Queensland and its dependencies and Vice-Admiral of same etc – stripped of his assets.

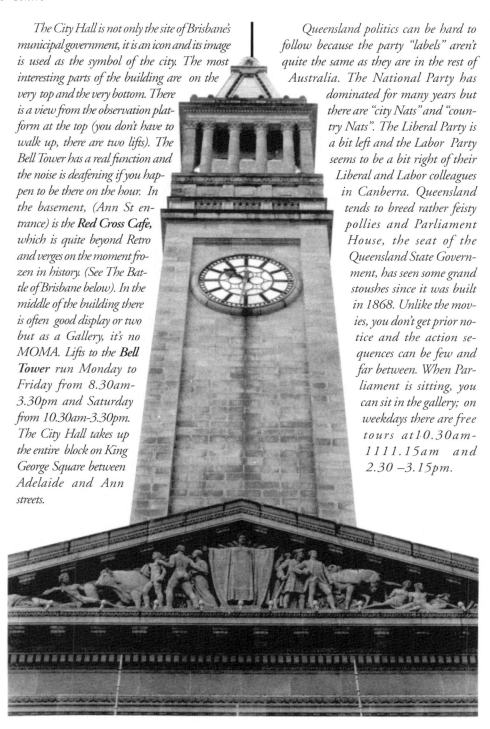

The City Hall is not only the site of Brisbane's municipal government, it is an icon and its image is used as the symbol of the city. The most interesting parts of the building are on the very top and the very bottom. There is a view from the observation platform at the top (you don't have to walk up, there are two lifts). The Bell Tower has a real function and the noise is deafening if you happen to be there on the hour. In the basement, (Ann St entrance) is the **Red Cross Cafe,** which is quite beyond Retro and verges on the moment frozen in history. (See The Battle of Brisbane below). In the middle of the building there is often good display or two but as a Gallery, it's no MOMA. Lifts to the **Bell Tower** run Monday to Friday from 8.30am-3.30pm and Saturday from 10.30am-3.30pm. The City Hall takes up the entire block on King George Square between Adelaide and Ann streets.

Queensland politics can be hard to follow because the party "labels" aren't quite the same as they are in the rest of Australia. The National Party has dominated for many years but there are "city Nats" and "country Nats". The Liberal Party is a bit left and the Labor Party seems to be a bit right of their Liberal and Labor colleagues in Canberra. Queensland tends to breed rather feisty pollies and Parliament House, the seat of the Queensland State Government, has seen some grand stoushes since it was built in 1868. Unlike the movies, you don't get prior notice and the action sequences can be few and far between. When Parliament is sitting, you can sit in the gallery; on weekdays there are free tours at 10.30am-1111.15am and 2.30 –3.15pm.

The Customs House (1849)

At 399 Queen Street, right on the banks of the Brisbane River, on one of the best bits of real estate in the city, stands the **Brisbane Customs House**, It is probably the most graceful old building in Brisbane but it still doesn't have a proper job. Owned by the University of Queensland, it currently houses a small private collection of Australian paintings and some fine Chinese pottery in the **Customs House Gallery.**

They nicked the dome idea from London's St Pauls and over the years it has survived the threat of demolition, termite infestation, builders' extensions, extra storeys, additional wings, and many suggested "improvements". It was finally restored to perfection by the University. It now houses the charming **Customs House Brasserie** (see 10 EAT AND DRINK) where you can sit outside, by the River and, over a glass of wine, try to think up ways that this fine building might one day fulfil its potential.

Late for work

Botanic Gardens

Unlike the larger cities of Sydney and Melbourne which are taking on a more international look, Brisbane still has a distinctive local style and you are reminded of it all over the city. People still seem to find time to meet on street corners and the gardens are filled with poinsettias, bougainvilleas, and jacarandas. While in the streets you can find giant rainforest trees and lines of great palm trees.

In most cities, botanic gardens tend to be in the oldest part of town and are usually very much part of its history. **The Botanic Gardens** in Brisbane are no exception. Beside the River and marking the spot of the settlement's first vegie patch, it is also the site of the elaborately festooned landing pontoon set up to greet the new Governor of Queensland in 1859. (Its modern equivalent, the 10,000 capacity **River Stage and Amphitheatre**, is now part of the Gardens complex).

The Brisbane **Botanic Gardens** remain an extension of the city in both style and content, rather than a separate international display. The **Mangrove Boardwalk**, the extraordinary **Finger Forest** and the majestic **rainforest** canopy all seem like an extension of this great tropical city. The Gardens were created by the first director/curator Walter Hill, who was given the task, the land and 500 pounds to get it going. It was the skills this gentleman applied in these gardens that introduced to Queensland the great agricultural produce synonymous with the state and which have burgeoned into major industries. Mangoes, pineapples, paw paws, custard apples, sugar cane, tobacco, ginger, coffee and many types of nuts and grapes – all came from the experimental work of Walter Hill in these city gardens. The Curator's Residence is now a charming **Cafe** and a great comfort stop from which to enjoy the environment of the Gardens. You can pick up a useful brochure with a wealth of detail on the gardens at the central rotunda.

THE BATTLE OF BRISBANE

During World War II, Brisbane was seen as Australia's first line of defence in the event of invasion from the north. This became a very real threat after the Japanese attack on Pearl Harbor in 1941. The British had surrendered Singapore and the Japanese air force had already bombed Darwin – the war was on our doorstep and the people of Brisbane were preparing for the "yellow peril" about to descend from the north.

Holidays were cancelled, sports were banned, transport was restricted, buildings were sand-bagged and concrete shelters lined the main streets. Milk and bread supplies were rationed, retail trading hours were shortened – even the traditional four to six o'clock swill in the pubs was threatened. All the different layers of Brisbane society were fused into a cohesive and single-minded homefront focussed on the job at hand – to hold fast the Brisbane line of defence at any cost.

Instead of the Japanese invasion, however, came the American invasion in the guise of "Liberators" or "Comrades in Arms". Two weeks after Pearl Harbor, the first division of American servicemen arrived in Brisbane. Initally, the city was relieved by their arrival, but as the ebullient GIs settled in, resentment built, particularly among the poorer paid Australian soldiers who envied the glamorous GIs swanning about, moving into their best buildings, taking out their girls and generally spoiling their turf. "Over-sexed, over-paid, and over here" was the common complaint.

No doubt the White Australia Policy, which was still in force, added tensions as the black GIs were segregated south of the Brisbane River while their white comrades stayed on the other side, enjoying the best of the city.

What follows is an extract from a paper by historian Helen Taylor, who quotes an Australian describing the events that took place in Brisbane on Thanksgiving Day 1942:

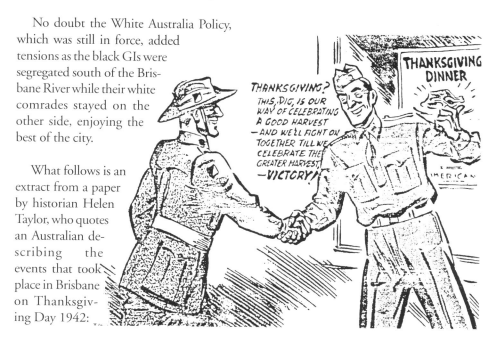

Hands off our shielas, mate.

The PX [on the corner of Creek and Adelaide streets] was a veritable Pandora's box, at that time off-limits to the Australian soldier. Australian servicemen were denied the right to a share of the "goodies", particularly the duty-free cigarettes. With American Military Police stoutly defending what Brisbane residents saw as an "Oasis of Plenty in a desert of Ration Books", the fracas soon widened. Servicemen of both countries vigorously defended "right" and "might". Civilians were caught up as the crowd or more than 2,000 surged into Queen Street. Summoned to the scene, the Australian Military Police removed their arm bands and moved into the crowd where they discharged their pent-up animosities over rightful possessions – women, beer and the run of the city.

Gun shots momentarily halted the melee as a panic stricken American Military Policeman at the PX discharged his rifle, killing one Australian soldier and wounding seven others as well as a civilian bystander. Next, "All hell broke loose". Only the timely arrival of the fire brigade and the good offices of the local police, the crush of the crowd and the possibility of "better fun elsewhere" quelled the hostility of those gathered. The shattered PX and the wrecked trams remained a monument to the violence, if not hatred, of a moment of November madness.

To the crowds that spilled from Hoyts Regent, in Queen Street, at 7.45 pm on that humid November night in 1942, Queen Street resembled a war zone. Tram and cars were overturned, signs uprooted, wounded Australian and American servicemen everywhere. They had just seen the movie *Mrs Miniver*, starring Greer Garson. The Vicar's final words in the movie were: *This is the people's war! It is our war! We are the fighters! Fight it, then. Fight it with all that is in us and may God defend the right.*

CITY DOINGS

The streetscape of the city is dominated by the high clean lines of shiny glass structures conceived in the past decade, and mellowed by comely, befitting sandstone edifices that reflect the pomp of the Victorian era. Even the CBD in Brisbane has a relatively, relaxed, easy, bush style that blends well with a newfound urban confidence. Those who live and work in the city of Brisbane seem to find a comfortable balance between work and play and seem genuinely happy to be there.

Heritage Trails

The Brisbane City Council Heritage Unit has put together a set of walking trails. There are 10 walks, but some of them can also be drives. **The City Centre Trail** starts at King George Square at the City Hall and moves past the wonderful Victorian Gothic Revival **Albert Street Uniting Church**. A little farther on is the vast former People's Palace, built by the Salvation Army in 1911 and now the fine **Palace Backpackers'** (6 PLACES TO STAY). Toward the end of the City Trail, in George Street is **The Mansions**, built around 1890 to an unusual design thought to suit local climatic conditions. On the corner of Roma and Ann streets, the **Carlton Crest Hotel** with its lavish cast-iron decorated verandas, is a fine example of hotel architecture. The **City Centre** and the **Brisbane Riverfront trails** can be combined into an excellent morning or afternoon. The rest of the trails are: the Brisbane Riverfront; New Farm (south and north); Fortitude Valley; Toowong Cemetery; Windsor; Hamilton; Wynnum to Manly; Latrobe and Given Terraces, Paddington. You can pick up detailed guides from the Brisbane Tourism booths at the **City Hall**, off King **George Square**, or in the **Queen Street Mall**.

In most cities, botanic gardens tend to be in the oldest part of town and are usually very much part of its history. The Botanic Gardens in Brisbane are no exception. Beside the River and marking the spot of the settlement's first vegie patch.

Albert Street Literary Walk has 32 brass plaques laid into the footpath with quotes about Brisbane from authors. The only problem is that you have to keep crossing the road as they are on both sides — be careful crossing.

The Red Cross Cafe

Those unique war days in Brisbane now live on only in the imagination and memory. There are a few tangible reminders, however. In the basement of the **Brisbane City Hall** is the **Red Cross Cafe** (Ann Street entrance). Staffed by volunteers, it is probably the last vestige of Brisbane's war years. The tea comes from a giant urn and the sandwiches and scones are made by the ladies of the Red Cross. Around the walls are photos of wartime Brisbane. Tea and scones around $2 and don't ask for a cappuccino.

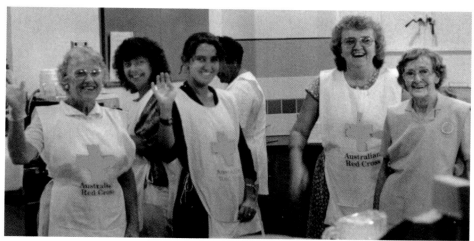

Beyond retro.

The great trend-setting real estate scam of 1848 (page 50) – the customers arrived on the good ship Fortitude.

4 North of the River

INCLUDES: The Great Land Scam of 1848; "Two to The Valley" for the food and pubs; Eddie's Chinatown; bikes and books at Newstead and New Farm; the old things of Paddington and the city within a city – University of Queensland.

The first account of the northern suburbs of Brisbane is in the notes of surveyor John Oxley who, in 1823s climbed Toorak Hill and, farther upstream, named Breakfast Creek as he went ashore near the site of the present hotel.

A trend-setting real estate salesman was the quirky Reverend John Dunmore Lang, a firebrand churchman and free-enterprise opportunist. In 1848 Lang sought out "a better class" of free settler to form the backbone of what he hoped would soon be called "Cooksland". And so in January 1849, in high summer, the *Fortitude* arrived from England with its cargo of eager migrants, who must have thought they'd been diverted to Hades. On arrival, there was no free land, no official welcome and certainly no chance of turning back. To these 256 souls it falls the honour (if without glory) of forming the first major intake to Brisbane of skilled free migrants.

SEVENTY FIVE YEARS LATER

"Two to The Valley!" would once get a couple to **Fortitude Valley** on a sixpenny tram ticket from Queen Street. The trams have gone (though they'll soon be back – watch our Updates on the Internet) and The Valley's great shopping emporia: T.C. Beirne, McWhirters, and Overells are gone or have passed their prime.

Fortitude Valley, a "community of corners" just three kilometres north of the CBD, has been in and out of the changing room to emerge another Soho?... Greenwich Village? King's Cross? Actually none and all of these. Quite simply, it is itself: The Valley. In the heritage-listed Post Office building on Wickham Street once hung a lifebuoy from the *Fortitude,* which set sail from Gravesend in September 1848 with Captain Christmas and those 256 free settlers on board, arriving in Brisbane four months later. It may symbolise the lifeline thrown to the district by the believers and business builders, mostly Chinese and Italians, after the Fitzgerald Inquiry's 1987 grilling of Fortitude Valley venues about the world's oldest profession.

Fortitude Valley has lowered its skirts (only slightly – strip joints and gay clubs light up **Wickham Street** and back-alley pros still linger along Brunswick Street), and dolled itself up into Brisbane's Oriental focal point, with **Chinatown Mall** and dragon festivals; a little Italy, with some of the best and cheapest cappuccino bars and pasta houses; and a bit of Ireland, centred on **Dooley's Hotel** (barmaids with brogue, Kilkenny ale and the St Patrick's Day parade). Renewed faith in The Valley as a cosmopolitan commercial centre with a bohemian character has brought a $350-million investment in residential, student and lifestyle developments in recent years.

So many of the new cafes and restaurants are popping up in this area that we have mentioned a number of them in case you get hungry while looking around. The very best of them are covered in more detail in 10 EAT AND DRINK, with the exception of the California Cafe, which is just as much a landmark as it is a place to get a good feed.

A good mix of hard-working people continued to move here and are still commemorated in the likes of the **California Cafe**, corner McLachlan and Brunswick streets. Here you can get a wharfie's breakfast – solid and fast – five sausages, three or four rashers of bacon, two grilled tomatoes, all covered in gravy with chips on top of that and two eggs crowning the lot. This place has been here so long that none of the employees know how old the cafe is. In 1952, at the age of 22, George Apostolos (left) bought the California Cafe. Decor is very retro without even trying, the result of a policy of "if it ain't broke don't fix it". Nothing has changed in those years except that the owner is now Lainey Loneragan, who can still cure your anorexia.

The kind of tucker that built Brisbane

There are a few good bookshops in the neighbourhood. Oddballs sporting a white Panama, fez, or a clean-shaven skull, browse shelves of '60s and '70s cinematic memorabilia stacked beside some of the best collections of Murri folklore and slightly off-the-wall exotica at **Books on Brunswick** 368 Brunswick Street. At **Red Books**, 350a Brunswick Street, has a selection of modern alternative culture books and a good bunch of novels. Girls and guys in trousers and skirts (respectively) flip through Linda Jaivin's *Confessions Of An S&M Virgin* and similar tomes.

In Ann Street between Brunswick and Duncan is a run of Retro shops – little shops of icon horror offerings, mostly '50s leftovers. **Kleptomania** and Bent are full of a selection of stuff, while **Scrabble** and **Honor Lulu** are more clothes shops with stuff. None stands out but together they are a good set. More on page 54. Wedged between these is the **Zoo**, a very laid-back alternative coffee/wine/ pool cafe with live music. Across the road is the **Fire-Works Gallery**, 678 Ann Street (More detail, 8 THE ARTS)and, if you need more art, The Valley boasts **The Art Circuit**, 17 art galleries (private) on the **Hail and Ride** bus route with runs every 15 minutes. If you don't like what you find, then there is not much of a wait. You can hop on and off the bus and browse over works from traditional paintings and woodblock prints to funky modern canvasses, elegant sculpture and delicate glassware. The ticket costs a few dollars and tours run daily through **The Valley** and adjacent suburbs of **New Farm** and **Newstead**. Information on **Trans Info** line: 13 12 30 (7 THINGS TO DO).

The Zoo takes our door prize.

*"I hope that no-one comes over to my house as a result of this book. The place is such a mess. I don't want anyone to make a fuss over me": **Merle Burton** (from <u>Two to the Valley</u>, by David Hinchcliffe and Dennis Bailey).*

Camp Row

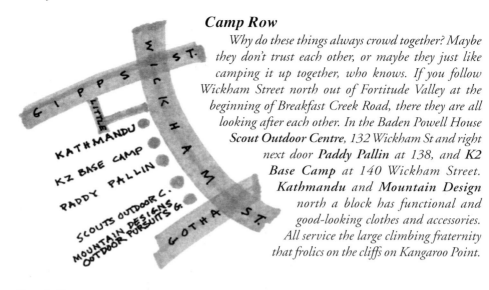

Why do these things always crowd together? Maybe they don't trust each other, or maybe they just like camping it up together, who knows. If you follow Wickham Street north out of Fortitude Valley at the beginning of Breakfast Creek Road, there they are all looking after each other. In the Baden Powell House **Scout Outdoor Centre**, *132 Wickham St and right next door* **Paddy Pallin** *at 138, and* **K2 Base Camp** *at 140 Wickham Street.* **Kathmandu** *and* **Mountain Design** *north a block has functional and good-looking clothes and accessories. All service the large climbing fraternity that frolics on the cliffs on Kangaroo Point.*

Funk Street

Red Books, *A smallish shop at 350a Brunswick Street, has a selection of "Modern Alternative" culture books and a good bunch of novels – next to the groovy* **Bitch Cafe**. **Books on Brunswick** *which is a more traditional bookshop with helpful staff and a good selection of "allsorts", 368 Brunswick Street. Both bookshops close to the mall. In Ann Street between Brunswick and Winn streets. There is a run of "Retro" shops with a good variety of clothes and fossickables.* **Kleptomania & Bent**, *705 Ann Street, is full of things, more of a selection;* **Scrabble** *at 717 Ann Street and* **Honor Lulu** *at 715 are more clothes shops with stuff. None really stands out dramatically but they are a good set. Next to Honor Lulu is* **Trash Video**, *a good store specialising in classic cult films. Wedged between these is the* **Zoo**. *A very laid back alternative coffee/wine/pool cafe with live music. More on the Zoo in 8 ARTS & SHOWS*

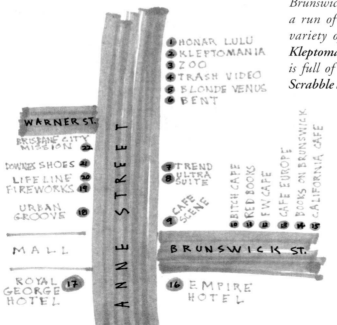

1 HONAR LULU
2 KLEPTOMANIA
3 ZOO
4 TRASH VIDEO
5 BLONDE VENUS
6 BENT

WARNER ST.
BRISBANE CITY MISSION 22
DOWNES SHOES 21
LIFE LINE 20
FIREWORKS 19
URBAN GROOVE 18

7 TREND
8 ULTRA SUITE
9 CAFE SCENE
10 BITCH CAFE
11 RED BOOKS
12 FW CAFE
13 CAFE EUROPE
14 BOOKS ON BRUNSWICK
15 CALIFORNIA CAFE

ANNE STREET
MALL
ROYAL GEORGE HOTEL 17

BRUNSWICK ST.
16 EMPIRE HOTEL

Brunswick Street Markets in the **Brunswick Street Mall** is a pretty big deal in the Valley on Saturday mornings. There's a stage midway for good bands – nothing too one way or the other, but sophisticated stuff tailored to the mood, and the buskers are pretty good, too. Coffee shops everywhere, including **Societe** where you can get a big bowl of latte (Betty Blue style) and **Fat Boys** for very funky coffee and dining outside, inside or underground. Tuesday nights at 8 pm, true cult movies, not just old ones, and they're all pretty good. The **Royal George Hotel** has tables on the street for a quiet lunch-time ale and the usual pub scene.

When do get my ice-cream?

You can cut through an alley to the **Burlington Supermarkets,** in the T. C. Beirne Centre, Chinatown Mall. Brunswick Street Markets incorporates the **Chinatown Markets,** which are a bit thin. **McWhirters**, with a very spacious, clean indoors centre is not so much a market as a shopping centre with market-style shops and bargain stores, including **Geeta** – Indian, Island, Fijian and South African and South American groceries. Lots of goodies to dig around in and a big car park next door, with overhead walkway to get from car park to McWhirters.

Brunswick Street is also a *loca bellissima* for Italian nosh. **Mellino's** garlic gnocchi and cacao coffee, Giardinetto's fettuccine di mare, a dish of Moreton Bay bugs doused in brandy and tomato cream. Contrast this with the quick coldie and counter lunch at the **Royal George** on Brunswick, The Valley's oldest (and looking it) surviving hotel, built in 1854, or the Empire on Ann Street, the **Prince Consort** on Wickham (getting a $40-million dust-off), or the **Wickham on Wickham,** a loud night-time Mecca popular with gays and lesbians. All, though, are still dressed up in wrought iron lace – the hotels, we mean.

Eddie Liu, the father of Chinatown.

CHINATOWN

Half a block south of Brunswick you're in the **Chinatown Plaza,** which the then Lord Mayor Sallyanne Atkinson opened in 1987 by stroking two large lion statues. It was renovated later and launched with a celebration on Chinese new Year's Eve hosted by Lord Mayor Jim in a coolie's hat. A choice of 22 Asian restaurants in one location, the **Autumn Moon Festival, Hung Phat's** jade jewellery (diamonds set while you wait), and **Wing Hing's** fascinating herb, acupuncture and medicine shop. Try Barbara Harman's "Have Chopsticks Will Wander" tour.

Eddie Liu carries a card saying: Honorary Ambassador for the City of Brisbane. Edward Liu, OBE. "When I came here in 1942, there was only one high-rise building – the TNT building. Oh gosh, I've been here too long. I've been in Australia since 1937." In 1942, Eddie was the secretary of the Seamen's Union. He seems shy about this period – probably because he had power – and when asked about any strife in that time, he just shakes his head and changes the subject. "In 1973 I had a Chinese herbal practice, which I ran until 1986." During that time the then clubhouse of the Chinese Club, Dixon Street, was flooded in the "Seventy-four big one". "The water was two inches from the ceiling. I suppose by that time I was hooked as a Valley person when Russ Hinze, you know Russ [controversial state government minister for local government during the Bjelke Petersen years] he asked me to join a special committee to look at the plan for China Town." It was opened in January 1987 and Eddie calls this "the happiest day of my life".

The Enjoy Inn, corner Duncan and Wickham St Fortitude Valley, is Eddie's top spot for Chinese tucker. Another Chinatown recommendation is cha-siu-lom-mein (barbecue pork and noodles) from either the **Burlington BBQ** or the **New Wing Hing BBQ** – the chap who cooks here says that you cannot spell the name of this dish in English because it is different in four or five parts of China and there is only one England!

A bit farther north on Wickham Street is **SMA** (Steel My Art), 622 Wickham Street, a family concern that started by selling handmade metal "things" on the market circuit. Mimi and Michael, with Mimi's sister Donna and nephew Sean, all work at the back of the shop to create original work and sometimes modifications to imports. The imports mostly come from Java. Major items as well as fossickables.

Steel My Art – if you can.

NEW FARM

Today in New Farm older locals cling to their Italian heritage; their street chatter is thick Napoli, while the shops and street cafes overflow with young trendies bubbling in Aussie, Kiwi, British and American artspeak. You'll also find a few Welsh, though.Quaint tree and cafe-lined streets such as Merthyr and Llewellyn remind us that taffies Henry Matthews, Richard Jones and Sir Samuel Griffith built estates here. Sam boyo, bought a lot of New Farm in 1870 and went on to become Queensland Premier, Chief Justice and chief architect of the Constitution that brought the Commonwealth of Australia into being in 1901.

New Farm is the prime riverfront address and often judged Brisbane's most livable suburb with easy access to the city by ferry, bus or bike. Traditional housing culture, multi-million-dollar development, a cosmopolitan mix of people and lively cafe culture have made it the darling of the urban renewal push. New Farm was Brisbane's first suburb to be part of a major $13-million City Council suburban centre improvement program.

The family tree.

New Farm Deli on Brunswick. Vince and Maria Anello and Teddy and Lisa Tarabay (above) serve up a great Hero (pastrami, cheese, bacon bits, lettuce, tomato, artichoke, cue and mayo) or the Great Italian (pesto, provolone cheese, pan-fried eggplant and tomato).

They won the inaugural CSR Coffee Shop of the Year award. In the cafe, Vince will seat you inside, outside, or across the drive in the pagoda outside the post office for wonderful pre-prepared foccacia and a most excellent coffee. Very busy at lunch. 900 Brunswick Street, Sun-Thurs, 7am–6pm; Fri–Sat 7am till late.

The deli can stock you up for a picnic you can take down the end of Brunswick Street to New Farm Park gates open at 5am and close Mon–Thus at 7pm; Fri–Sun at 9pm for vehicle access, otherwise is open 24 hours a day. A loop, one way around, is flat and good for bicycling, with plenty of shade under the jacaranda and fig-lined avenues. Backing on to Merthyr Croquet Club is the most beautiful **New Farm Park Kiosk**, a tea room with, we believe, as yet unrealised potential. Sit and enjoy your tea and scones in a grandiose rotunda-style structure that blends wonderfully with the Moreton Bay figs, a feature of this park.

New Farm Park

Right on the River with its own wharf at the end of Brunswick Street. The River CityCats stop here.

Michael Gambaro gave us mudcrabs. His son Johnny owns **Rosati's** on the Park at 938 Brunswick, which is a magnet for smart business chicks who crave the seafood pasta linguini with clams and a bottle of Antonori Orvietto Italian white, all for a reasonable set price. Jean-Pierre and Susan Buret change the flavour at the **Continental Cafe,** 21 Barker Street, with Moroccan braised chicken and couscous pilaf – and don't forget the vanilla bean and burnt caramel ice cream by the scoop. Which brings us to Michel Thompson's **Le Scoops,** the Paddo favourite, that has also opened at the Aix cafe-bistro at 83 Merthyr Road. The Aix Caesar is great...so too is the open kangaroo tartlet with wild mushrooms and juniper

The New Farm (enchanted) Park.

beurre blanc or the take-your-breath-away zucchini and garlic pizza.

Down to **Fishface,** Carlo and Sylvia Disano's 7-day BYO at 85 Merthyr Road, for the Big Stuff, a Snogging Rex Hunt fish of the day or Currumbin cazbah, a quail stuffed with polenta and dates and served with champagne and grapefruit sauce and a stack of sweet potatoes. The fish are jumpin' to live jazz 1.30pm–4.30pm Sundays. Bookings essential. Try also ... the **Moray Cafe** 158 Moray Street for a whopping Eggs Benedict or Moray burger of Tandoori chicken pattie, char-grilled with rahita and mango chutney; Gay McCosker's **Eve's on the River**, 25/53 Vernon Terrace with its interesting pottery art; **Wok on Inn** Oodles of Noodles Bar, 728 Brunswick ... beef and chicken, or try the seafood combination; the **Flour Shop**, 21C Barker Street, joined to a flower shop that sells very special flowers. People come from everywhere for both. (Across the road is the excellent Village Twin Cinema).

At 79 James Street, **The Purple Olive** BYO is noted for Mediterranean influences. **Sahibs** and **Sitar** for Indian, both on Brunswick; **Koffies Espresso Bar** open 7 days, 726 Brunswick; the best Italian pastry at **Savoia Pasticceria** gelateria caffe, Merthyr Village; **Amigos** for authentic South American and Afro Latin cuisine, 3/79 James Street; top pub grub at **The Queens Arms Hotel** on James Street with the social set mingling with Rupert Murdoch's journalists.

DIG (Directions In Gardens) Shop, 4/154 Merthyr Road (above), James Turner has a smallish selection of beautiful upmarket garden ornaments and plants and all the help you need. He has planters and candlesticks and such, copied from classical designs and remade locally out of reconstituted stone. Some very good garden and landscaping books.

Position, position, position. **Gerties**, corner Barker and Brunswick Streets has got it. Good and cheap breakfasts, set combos from tea or coffee and muffins though tea and coffee with cereal/muesli to the full catastrophe. Nice modern atmosphere with big windows on the corner to the street. They do other meals, too.

Our researcher had more coffees and focaccia than he could stomach, then spotted a pie shop and headed for the **Gum Nut Bakery,** 874 Brunswick Street. A big puffy CWA (Country Women's Association) type lamington looked irresistible before a muscular sweet pie took his eye. "Is that apple?" "Do you want apple or apricot?" "Apricot please". She gave a wink and went out the back and came back with a pie that looked the same and said: "This one was baked at lunch, these ones out front are old." "How old?" "They were baked this morning". The cost? Less than $2 for a pie that could cost twice as much in Melbourne or Sydney. They (Ross, Annette and Ann Weston) have taken the good old suburban cake shop and beefed it up. "Nothing fancy here, love."

A BIT FARTHER NORTH

If you are in the mood for steak and beer, go no farther than the **Breakfast Creek Hotel** Sandgate Road, Albion. A good pub atmosphere and old ghosts of the Left. This is where the Australian Labor Party had its national convention for many years. Fourex and Victoria Bitter are on tap in the public bar, though the popularity of the local brew seems to have slipped in a major way in recent years. To get there, just head for the airport on Route 25 and park your hog out the back.

"A pot of beer"

Breakfast Creek Wharf across the Creek from the Hotel, should not be considered for the inappropriate gondolas, touristy restaurants or the Bicentennial Water Clock. But it is worth going to for the fish-and-chip shop. Glenn Miller from Abtour nominates **The Fish Market** as the best in Brisbane. Don't just ask for fish and chips, because you'll have to specify your fish preference.

North West

The Park Road Cafe Strip, Milton. There is somewhere in the world all these people sitting along the Park Road cafe strip would rather be, say Milan, Rome, the Champs Elysées or The Boat House in NY but we don't think it's here. The coffee is pretty good but the food is – how do we say – hurried, though not expensive. Just ignore the 6-metre Eiffel tower with purple bougainvillea dripping down. The clothes are beautiful, the cars are beautiful, the people are beautiful and my hair is a mess. Behind these places in a small arcade is **Pamela's Pantry,** which sells exquisite pantry food, pies jams, pickles and a lot more. Take away a cookie or fare for a whole dinner party. They stock the Australian cooler bag **Didgeridoona** a portable cooler bag made of Drizabone-type canvas with leather handles and insulated with Australian wool – it works like a sheep. A must for the plonk porter, (11 THINGS TO BUY).

Unless it's a Ferrari, leave it out the back.

Coaldrake's bookshop 8/ 32 Park Road, Milton. Guy Coaldrake's two nicely laid out stores are across an arcade. When we called there, an elderly lady came in and declared: "I only need one book to read." Needless to, say Guy was able to help her.

You can get a good view of all the Park Road colour and movement across the road, inside or out at the **Arrivederci Pizza al Metro**, 1 Park Road Milton. They serve home-style pizza, expensive up against the super deals of the chains but worth every fatty, dribbly cheesy mouthful. They also provide a home-delivery service.

Or **Cafe Nero,** 1 Park Road, Milton, has butcher's paper and a little pot of crayons on each table to entertain kids but the waitress says: "Two out of three kids don't use them but all the adults do." The food is fresh and there's plenty of it.

Mountain Province, 21 Park Road, Milton. Exotic antique furniture and tribal artefacts – expensive but beautiful. Just off Park Road is the **Douglas Street Design Centre,** 46 Douglas Street, a very stylish decorator centre with a number of shops, all home-based, each with its own specialty. Antique and Country, Brisbane Plantation Shutters, Corso de' Fiori (very modern furniture), Cuffe and Good (antiques and jewellery), Design Warehouse, Ironwood (antique wooden furniture), Karavan (oriental carpets), La Chantelaina (wall art), Leadlight Creation, Metal Art Design, Tezzere Tiles and Mezzedes cafe and restaurant to contemplate all the money you've just spent or wish you could. On the corner of Douglas and Camford Street is **Heritage Editions,** with a huge selection of exquisite prints and, up steep stairs, if you are game, original maps and prints at the **Antiquarian Print Gallery**, Camford Square, Camford Street (near Douglas Street, Milton). You'll need plenty of time on this one as there is a lot to browse through.

San Rocke, patron saint of the sick.

TENERIFF AND NEWSTEAD

Watch this space. This is a place that will be very grand in 20 years. Formerly a working industrial area, now desperately trying to gentrify, it already has apartments, cafes, galleries and shops. More than 2000 trees were planted at New Farm and Teneriffe Hill between 1995 and 1997. On-road bike lanes link the State Government **Safe Bikeway** at Wilson Outlook with bike lanes along Moray Street and Oxlade Drive to New Farm as well to Teneriffe ferry terminal. Eventually, when the 3.5 km riverside promenade between New Farm and Newstead Park is completed, cyclists will be able to pedal between the city and Breakfast Creek.

When the rest of the maritime buildings are converted to hotels and apartments there will be people to use the River walks that go for many kilometres and Brisbane will have come of age as a city. This area gives a hint of what Brisbane could and will be. A shopping browse "must" is **Scotts New Farm Antiques Centre**, 85 Commercial Road, Newstead. It is a market-style centre with lots of stalls under one roof. For $35, in Shop 33, a National Party of Queensland poster proclaims "Keep Queensland in front, Vote for Joh Bjelke Petersen". More shops of all descriptions – everything from bakers' tables to a collection of lead soldiers that would make a collector cry, Mon-Fri 10am– 5pm; Sat-Sun 9am–5pm. Also **Chelsea Antiques**, 32 Vernon Terrace, Teneriffe Wharf, is a big multi-level warehouse with a large selection of more traditional antiques from furniture to smaller pieces.

The junction of Petrie Terrace and Caxton Street (above) is thick with bars and restaurants. At the top is **Lord Alfred (LA) Hotel**, an upmarket young bar; **Casablanca**, a charcoal grill with a South American flavour with all the waiting staff wearing kilts. Why? Why not! A little farther on, **The Caxton Hotel**, Caxton Street. Lively atmosphere with good food, best out the back in the garden. These are the places to go when other places are closing down. On the LA Hotel side is **Trattoria di Santa Patata** (BYO), 19 Caxton Street. Live opera singing with piano on Saturday nights, a beautiful atmosphere to dine. A very classy spot, book well in advance. For those who are that way inclined there's **The Irish Connection**, 25 Caxton Street. Vanessa McCready will serve you a Guinness and an Irish dish (not her).

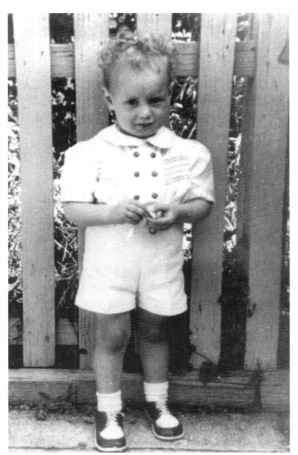

NORTH WEST

Paddington Antique Centre, 167 Latrobe Terrace, is where you can start your browse around the Antique Circuit (details, 11 THINGS TO BUY).

As well as Paddington, Bardon, Red Hill and Ashgrove make a nice free-range tour for hardened browsers – there is just so much of it. It's hard to find a starting point – it depends on where you're coming from. The buses run around these suburbs, so if you need to check the timetable on **TransInfo** 13 12 30 (operates 24 hours).

Rosebank Cottage, 210 Musgrave Road, Red Hill is also a good place to start. A portrait of the founder, William White (left) as a young boy hangs on the wall. Well-crafted waxed and stencilled country furniture. (See details, 11 THINGS TO BUY).

MoreThings in the North West

Tucked on a bend of Latrobe Terrace (blink and you'll miss it) is **Jazzworks**. Greg Quigley has all the good oil, 54 Latrobe Terrace. A comprehensive range of hard-to-get sheet music. Sharing the shop is **B and C Woodwind & Brass Studio** and even if you don't play, you can just look and enjoy. **Sweethearts Cafe**, 161 Latrobe Terrace, has movie nights, as well as the cafe stuff. Three-course movie menu (around $22) Dial M... Some Like It Hot, Key Largo – you get the picture, and prizes for the film quiz winners. **Bardon Fine Foods**, 72 MacGregor Terrace, will give you, arguably and proudly boasting, the best hamburger in Brisbane. After the burger, ask for 45 grams of Moonstone Cookie made by **Why Not Cookies.** Yum. Forget the burger. **Cornucopia**, 88 Latrobe Terrace, open daily. A multi-culti deli that does lunch and brekkie with home-made porridge and cereals. And **Le Scoops**, 283 Given Terrace, is legendary for frappes or home-made ice-cream.

Hand Made Things, 33 MacGregor Terrace Bardon. Some interesting things you may not have seen, some you won't want to. Wish powder, do-it-yourself limb repair kit (with stick) and coat-hangers with bosoms, or a brazier (metal basket to hold heat beads – see right) to warm you when you just can't give up the verandah life as it gets cold in the winter months.

Mary Ryan, 179 Latrobe Terrace, is one of an ever-expanding selection of branches. An excellent bookshop plus food and the coffee in the cafe. The cafe is lined with author posters – most of them signed – and is under the shop looking over a lovely garden path leading to a pagoda. They organise literary club nights in conjunction with the *Courier Mail*.

Namaste, 93a Musgrave Road, Red Hill. Lloyd Magdalinski deals with 52 Nepalese families buying and importing to Brisbane. Lovely leather, good-quality clothes – not the usual market stuff. Dalai Lama and buddhist supplies, and hand-made paper using methods that are centuries' old.

University of Queensland

This is not just a university, it's rather like a town within a city with its theatres and cinemas, museums, sportsgrounds, cafes and one of the best bookshops in Brisbane. Founded in 1910 in order to celebrate the anniversary of Queensland's separation from the colony of New South Wales, the St Lucia campus was established on 114 hectares of farmland, on a bend in the river – an enjoyable ferry ride from the centre of Brisbane. The University is now one of Australia's largest and most respected and the St Lucia campus has many surprises (see 7 THINGS TO DO).

High and dry in Manly.

5 South of the River

INCLUDES: From dockland past to the Arts; home of Brisbane's most culturally diverse suburb, West End, and to the seaside towns for nostalgia and fish and chips.

From the time of white settlement, the River divided Brisbane into two separate villages, the characteristics of each being quite distinctive. Those differences, both social and topographic, set the style of the suburbs south of the River and would underpin the changes in both areas as they developed. Initially topography was the deciding factor. Brisbane is a sub-tropical region and is susceptible to flooding. As a result, the best spots in town were those on the peaks of the surrounding areas, and the flats were taken by cheaper housing and industry. There is more high ground north of the River so more status applied there in the early days. There was also the open-drain sewerage issue. If you lived on the bottom of the hill or even halfway down, you collected the effluent from your haughtier neighbours. Mind you, there were pockets of grandeur south of the river in high-ground areas of West End and Highgate Hill.

The differences between north and south of the River were exaggerated with time and in 1888, South Brisbane became a separate municipality. By 1903 it had become a separate city, but by 1925 the civic leaders of the south had thought better of it and moved back into the fold as part of Greater Brisbane. *"...the bush twang of stockwhip and bullock yokes"* is a somewhat romantic description of activities on the southern bank of the Brisbane River in the early 1800s. It told of the days when bullock drivers and squatters brought in their produce from the surrounding Darling Downs, when the wool boats would be stacked up in the River. When their turn came to load, they would tie up to trees around where the Queensland Performing Arts Complex is now.

By the late 1800s, the main action on the southern bank better fitted the description of a tarts and arts town. Brisbane's busiest port had not only developed on the south bank, but it had also created the need for a playground for itinerant gold diggers and dock workers.

Sly grog shops, pubs and brothels were the dominant commercial interests and it was well recognised as the main "red light" district. It became Brisbane's main entertainment centre with the town's first theatres, Croft's Amphitheatre, the Cremorne and the Bohemia being built there. It was this latter function – most certainly not the former, we hasten to add – that made the south bank an appropriate site for the entertainment tradition to be perpetuated and crystallised into its contemporary form at the opening in April 1985 of the glamorous, comprehensive and quite proper **Queensland Performing Arts Complex.**

From the days of earliest settlement, the Murries had been confined to the south bank, well away from the "respectable" white settlers, who preferred to be to the north. Overt acts of racism continued into contemporary times and in WWII, black American servicemen were segregated from their white comrades and confined to the south of the river with (unofficially, of course) their own brothels, serviced largely by Murri women.

David Malouf, Brisbane's literary treasure, grew up in South Brisbane and his lightly veiled autobiographical *Johnno* set in those wartime years, reveals his bias for the area. *"... My memories were all of our old house in South Brisbane, with its wide latticed verandahs, its damp mysterious storerooms where sacks of potatoes and salt had been kept in the ever dark, its washtubs and copper boiler under the porch, its vast garden that ran right through to the street behind, a wilderness that my grandfather, before he died, had transformed into a suburban farmlet, with rows of spinach, tomatoes, lettuce, egg plants, a shed where onions and garlic hung from the rafters, and a wire coop full of fowls. The new house in Hamilton was stuffy and pretentiously over-furnished and depressingly modern."*

The few contemporary reminders of this period include the dry dock at the **Maritime Museum** in Dock Street, South Brisbane, and some old pylons still visible along the River bank near the **Captain Cook** (Freeway) **Bridge**. Now the divisions between north and south aren't as marked of course, and there's a different feeling south of the river. A feeling of expectation. The tarts have moved out but the Arts are coming into their prime. (See 8 THE ARTS).

South Bank Parkland

The Parklands are a very well-crafted, well-landscaped inner city escape. Immediately post Expo '88 this place was a dust bowl, with the pub standing alone like the last car in the lot waiting for a new owner. City Beach, now one of the main area's features, has white sands and filtered water and is sealed off from the River. Buskers pitch at the main entrance (below) to the Beach and there is usually some excellent talent; you are unlikely to see the same act twice. After removing himself from a straitjacket in under 60 seconds (59 to be exact) Amazing Ashley told us that South Bank is on his international circuit and is a must on the yearly itinerary (we didn't know they took it so seriously). A blackboard keeps you informed about the acts on time, and in line.

South Bank Butterfly House

It contains the world's largest collection of live Australian butterflies. Downstairs are the bugs, insect giants and spiders (the really good ones are behind bullet-proof glass). Open 8am–5pm. (More detail, 7 THINGS TO DO).

The concessions at South Bank Parklands are not as expensive as you might expect. There is not much of a choice, although **Captain Snapper** has good value fish and chips with a dozen oysters at the restaurant for less than $10, and there are plenty of excellent picnic spots not to feed the seagulls in. **Chez Laila** at the Maritime Museum end of South Bank is a good, reasonably priced cafe with Lebanese influenced food.

A weighty responsibility

The **Nepalese Temple (Nyatpola Pagoda)** stands regally overlooking the River. Originally built by King Mala to combat his recurring troubled dreams, in a land far away (for reasons only he knows). APAC (**Association to Preserve Asian Culture**) is jointly responsible with the **BCC** (Brisbane City Council) and other corporate sponsors, for this raw wood masterpiece. Or is it just a big "thing"? A small plaque nearby reads "May peace prevail on Earth." A leftover from Expo 88, it is one of those things you would not normally see unless you travelled to Nepal.

South Bank Craft Markets

These markets are a bit touristy with a mix of run-of-the-mill market crafts and imports, with the psychics, masseurs and palm-readers scattered throughout. (See detail, 11 THINGS TO BUY).

WEST END

Still Brisbane's most culturally diverse suburb, West End (not 'The') was the toehold in The Great Australian dream for many waves of non-Anglo immigrants. It was known to its indigenous owners as *Kurilpa* – "place of rats" – a probable reference to the water rats that inhabited the nearby River and surrounding lowland swamps.

After white settlement here, the first population to add to the ethnic diversity were Irish. **St Francis' Church** (Dornoch Terrace) and **St Mary's** (Merivale and Peel streets) are the Catholic reminders of this period. In the late 1890s, Greek, Cypriot and Lebanese immigrants began arriving in Australia and large numbers settled in South Brisbane/West End. House names like *Kithera* and *Cedars* remain as evidence of this era, but the clearest indication is in the business and retail strips, where accountants, solicitors, tailors, shops and delis have signage in Greek script. **Cyprus House** (Jane Street), **AHEPA Hall** and the **Hellenic Building** (Boundary Sreet) are evidence of the strength of Greek settlement here. Modern buildings like the **Greek Orthodox Church** of St George, **Hellenic House** and the **Greek** school are located in Edmondstone, Browning and Russell Street. The Lebanese **Maronite Church** is nearby in Ernest Street.

The social make up of this near-city residential and industrial suburb is further enhanced by a number of large backpacker hostels and older style boarding houses. This district also has a history of bohemian or left-wing populations. Extremely active community organisations and social protest campaigns on broader community access and equity issues regularly have their beginnings here.

Time out in West End.

The **Kurilpa Public Library** and **Kurilpa Kindergarten** in Boundary Street, West End, reflect the traditional indigenous name for the area. There is still a large Murri population in the West End/South Brisbane area. **Musgrave Park** (between Edmonstone, Cordelia and Russell St) is a large parkland with special significance to Brisbane's Murri people. It is an open space used for celebration, confrontation, protest and gatherings. Local Murries have often called for the establishment of a permanent indigenous cultural centre here. These requests are usually met by howls of protest from other users of the parkland, especially the Greek community, whose Community Centre faces the park from Edmonstone Street. The the annual **Paniyiri Festival** - a weekend celebration of Greek food, music, dancing and culture that is held in Musgrave Park.

Brisbane cafe society – West End style.

The rapidly changing character of the district with gentrification and large-scale residential and retail developments is a source of constant concern to its existing residents. The encroachment of commercial development and the continuing development of the South Bank Parklands site accentuates these changes. **West End** is on the cusp of transformation, yet despite this, it will always remain a resilient and diverse character suburb of Brisbane.

West End has many ethnicities fighting for domination and, as always, food is the battle bridge. The place to start is **Kim Tahnh**, 81 Vulture Street, for some of the best and cheapest croissants, bread, rolls and pastries, but you will need to get there early and wait in line. In the morning there is always a queue. Off for coffee now to **Cafe Babylon**, 142 Boundary Street which serves a fine brew to get you going and has a stylish decor to sit in and admire the neighbourhood, across the road is the **Avid Reader**, 173 Boundary a well laid out modern store. Fiona Stager (right) knows books and the local literary sceen. **Bent Books**, 205A Boundary Street. Open daily and until 9 pm on weekends. Has Brisbane's best selection of second-hand books, film scripts and sheet music Amadeus – to Zappa. Toward the end of the point is Hardgrave Road and not far up the hill on the corner is **Hong-Lan**, the best place locally for Asian groceries, 56 Vulture Street.

We'd rather be reading than weeding.

Mick's Nut Shop, 31 Hardgrave Street. A sign on the wall quotes a newspaper clipping from 1988: *By appointment. Mick's Nut Shop corner Hardgrave and Vulture St at West End – which specialises in fresh nuts – had some impressive customers yesterday. A chauffeur-driven limousine pulled up outside the shop and discharged two well-dressed women who said they wanted some macadamia nuts to take back to England. The pair were shopping for well known nut fanciers the Duke and Duchess of Kent, and had been recommended to Mick's.* Since 1970 this has been a popular family business and a smile is guaranteed. They have a range of nuts, dried fruits, and every legume imaginable.

British royalty shops here.

On the corner of Boundary and Mollison streets are two spots: **The Three Monkeys**, 58 Mollison Street, most astounding decor – Indian, Japanese, Nepalese, Indonesian. There are drapes, beads and every bohemian decoration you can imagine. A true den. All they need is a few old-style opium addicts. The garden continues the theme. Next door is the **Jazzy Cat**, 56 Mollison Street, a straighter version with a better range of food, though not as much fun.

King Ahiram's Lebanese, 88 Vulture Street – very quick and easy take-away, authentic and fresh. You may have to wait in line a bit in busy periods.

Lavender Blue Emporium, 61 Vulture Street (also at the Riverside Markets on Sunday). Everything from candles to cushions, pots to pastry stamps. No food here.

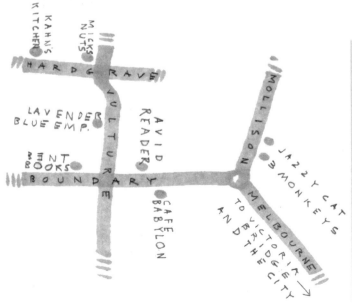

Up the hill, there's a strip of good cafes and restaurants. In the middle, **Khan's Kitchen**, an alfresco Pakistani restaurant – very cheap and fast, authentic and friendly. Kenneth Pervez (above), owner and chef is often seen out on the street chatting with patrons, 75 Hardgrave Street.

THE QUEENSLANDER

Up to and during the '20's areas of South Brisbane, Highgate Hill and West End were Brisbane's dress-circle residential locations. Today, streets around Dornoch Terrace at Highgate Hill still have some of Brisbane's grandest Queenslanders, facing north-east they looking down over the River and CBD. Some look to the east across the sweeping arches of the Gateway Bridge out to Moreton Bay; many of them are classified by the National Trust.

Historically, residential development in the South Brisbane/West End/Highgate Hill area followed the norm for the rest of Brisbane: large, grand, verandah-ringed Queenslander houses constructed on the crests of hills, along ridges and river banks to catch any cooling summer breeze. Traditionally, these homes occupied large blocks of land and were surrounded by established trees and gardens. Away from the River and in the hollows, timber workers' cottages were built on considerably smaller blocks.

To the Seaside

With the advent of industrial relations at the turn of the century, annual holidays and the growth of pubic transport, the pre-glitzy Surfers Paradise seaside suburbs of **Sandgate, Manly,** and **Wynnum** began to grow. Memories of these early beachside suburbs, which were about an hour out of town (now it's an easy half hour), are about feeding the seagulls, or taking about 35 minutes to go to a classic **Moreton Bay** spot where the tide goes out for ever. In 1911, Sandgate was the most popular of the beach destinations, but it's now bereft of most of its original charm. **The Fish Cafe** on Moreton Bay on the corner of the Esplanade and Cambridge Parade, **Manly,** has been serving fish and chips since the early 1920s. On Cambridge Parade, opposite **Manly Hotel** (which has jazz in the front garden on the weekend), is the **Harlequin Cafe** with big windows opening onto the street and a good breakfast. Also the **Pelicans Nest** on the Esplanade does a breakfast, as well as – you guessed it – fish and chips, but you can get it on a plate instead of wrapped in butcher's paper. There are many fish-and-chip shops to choose from and after extensive research (our cholesterol reached danger level) we pinpointed the **Wynnum Fish Markets,** 18 Fox Street. They buy fish from local fisherman and sell to the other fish-and-chip shops.

These places are strenuously resisting change and are appreciated by anyone nostalgic for the old-time Bayside.

High and dry in Manly.

Woolloongabba
(Murri for *Place of Whirling Water* or *Fight Talk Place*)

Traditionally a working-class area with links to shipbuilding and the railways, this rather forgotten strip is now bounded and bisected by major roads and the South-east Freeway. Sandwiched between the famous 'Gabba' (Brisbane Cricket Ground) and the infamous Ipswich Road (one of the main roads out of town) is a quiet haven dedicated to art, fine design, antiques and collectables. The **Woolloongabba Village** section of Logan Road is an inner-city block apparently forgotten by the road-wideners and demolishers – a street of architectural gems of 1860s to 1930s Brisbane – once the start of the Gold Coast Highway, which meandered through the southern suburbs of Brisbane down to Surfers Paradise. Find your way into this now almost land-locked street, and you'll also find some of Brisbane's finest spec-ialist antique stores and design studios. Most buses serving the south side of Brisbane still pass through Wooll-oongabba, so access by public transport is simple. From old French fruitwood chests to antique and colonial bric-a-brac and '50s shell lamps – all are here in a melange of shopfronts that orig-inally included an 1871 iceworks, a 1920s government office and a

Institute of sporting analysis.

1930s Chinese cafe. Along this street you can have a valuable oil painting restored, buy a grand William IV mirror for your ballroom, or watch internationally renowned master gilder **Sandy Bernside** applying gold leaf to treasures for dispatch worldwide. (Sandy has completed commissions for restoration on numerous major buildings, including Buckingham Palace.)

In the middle of this treasure trove there'll be somewhere you can find that special gift for the someone who has everything – like a redback spider or blowfly bowtie from the **Contemporary Art and Design Gallery** at 33 Logan Road. This interesting, ever-changing gallery specialises in promoting the works of local artists and craftspeople. Pineapple earings and brooches of endangered, indigenous frogs are a colourful Queensland treat. Over the road at No 16, in an 1860s sheet-metal and tin smithy workshop, is the **Contemporary Furniture Studio** (below). The showroom displays a range of furniture, lighting and useful or unusual items by local designers. (More detail, 11 THINGS TO BUY).

Cool off after bargain-hunting with a cold beer in the front bar of the famous Gabba Hotel (cnr Ipswich Road and Stanley Street), or wander 200m along Logan Road to the fabulously-restored **Broadway Hotel**. Built in 1906 in the Queen Ann style, this garishly painted "wedding cake" guards the corner of Logan and Wellington roads and also Balaclava Street.

Balaclava Street is home to wholesalers of pungent Indian spices and oriental culinary wonders, as well as jumbo Greek olives, nuts and goat cheese.

All things bright and beautiful.

The "ayes" have it.

Stones Corner

Farther along Logan Road, past a procession of car yards, at the junction of Old Cleveland Road, is the gentrifying suburban shopping strip of **Stones Corner**. Stones Corner in the '50s and '60s sold everything for the home dressmaker or housewife. In suburban decline through the '70s and '80s, but is now the home of trendy factory-direct samples and remaindered designer-name fashion clearance centres, as well as seconds china shops and giftwares. National brands (Country Road, Sportsgirl, Canterbury, Cue, etc) sit alongside trendy and not-so-trendy boutiques, gift shops, cafes and coffee shops. Aromas of freshly ground coffee and toasted focaccia waft across widened footpaths decorated with public sculpture and designer street furniture. Scattered throughout are some of the original shops: hardware, barber, snackbar (real laminex tables!), army disposals, tattooist and pawn shop. In the middle of all of this change is **Stones Corner Hotel**, a bastion of the former 6 o'clock swill, with the races blaring out onto the street and old men sunning themselves in doorways. Makeover and additions have not been kind to a once-grand watering-hole.

Stay.

This bustling suburban shopping centre, with more cappuccino machines than traffic lights, is a magnet for bargain-hunters and the smart set, while still serving the local community. Traffic calming and streetscape alterations have allowed footpath dining and pedestrians to reclaim the area from motor vehicles. Stones Corner is well served by public transport, but parking can be a problem at busy times (most times).

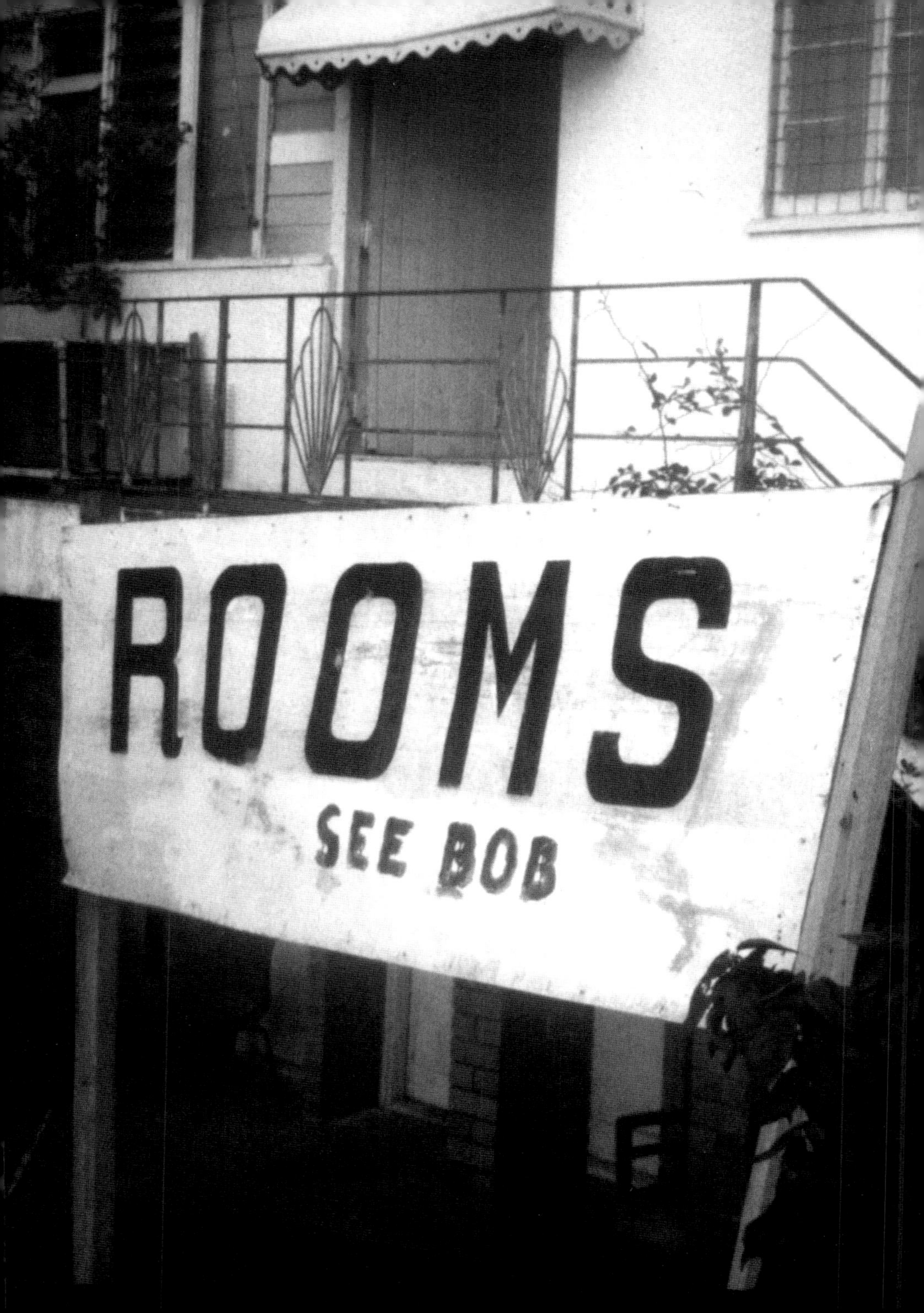
ROOMS
SEE BOB

6 Places to Stay

INCLUDES: From the "I really can't afford it, but I want something wonderful" to: "I want something wonderful but I have to watch the budget and "I want something wonderful but at a rock bottom price". A grand hotel and little personal ones; serviced apartments, guesthouses and backpacker hostels.

Untourists prefer places with local flavour and character. They are not keen on hotels or motels that present like international chains. Avoiding mass-market tourists is also important and they like to meet the locals and learn more about the best things to do from the source, rather than from a tour guide or brochure. So, where to stay is really the most important decision they can make, regardless of whether there is a little or a lot of money to spend.

For regular tourists it is relatively easy to choose accommodation because they tend to think vertically and trust in the stars. Meaning that it is easy to confuse price with quality and they think that the lower the price, the worse the accommodation. Or they confuse style with luxury – eg, they feel a four-star hotel is not as good as a five-star hotel.

We grade establishments in a different way. (See our criteria in The Guide to the Guide.) If an entry has a duck or two beside the name, then that means there is something extra special about it. If it has three, well that's close to heaven. Our Flying Ducks are awarded for inherent excellence and charm. The more ducks, the more inherent excellence and charm.

While Brisbane has plenty of accommodation, we found that at least for now, we can thoroughly recommend only 14 places to stay and only three of these are traditional hotels. The Heritage is, we believe, one of the best hotels in Australia and is given our top award of two flying ducks. The third hotel, the Conrad Treasury, is actually only a Clayton's recommendation. Odd? Well, we have our reasons...

Our symbolic use of $'s works as follows:

(per standard double, per night – note: rates during week are often very good value)

$	(cheap and good)	$15	-	$40
$$	(budget)	$40	-	$75
$$$	(moderate)	$75	-	$150
$$$$	(premium)	$150	-	$250
$$$$$	(top)	$250	-	up

It's worthwhile knowing that out of season, or for stays longer than a few days, you can usually negotiate a better tariff. And as you are booking direct rather than through a booking agency, there is more profit in your patronage for the owners of the establishments where you choose to stay.

Our categories of accommodation are hotels (traditional); apartment hotels; guesthouses/B&B's; backpackers.

HOTELS (traditional)

When you get into what we Australians call "five-star" hotels (which is usually a measure of their price and not necessarily their quality or style) they tend to be either American in style or European. To be an American five-star hotel usually means that they are overtly branded as part of an international chain and Hilton, Sheraton, etc, and they are all quite similar. This is done intentionally in order to comfort the weary traveller who doesn't want to encounter any idiosyncratic aspects on his (and it's usually "his") travels. Rather, he wants his accommodation to be a buffer to protect him from the threatening local environment. That's why all the glossy brochures look the same – as do the restaurants and the rooms and the waiters.

Though we have some sympathy with this concept, particularly in places such as Sarejevo or Phnom Penh, this type of hotel is not our bag. Rather we prefer the European five-star which is usually smaller (or appears that way), is often in an old building, and tends to be more style than luxury, more personal and less pretentious. Hotels where you are greeted with a simple "Good morning" rather than "Have a nice day". More important, in this type of hotel you rarely, only very rarely, sight a tour bus.

Two major new hotels in Brisbane have enabled the preservation of several of the city's rare remaining historical buildings – our top choice, **The Heritage**, incorporates the old Port Office, was built in 1880 in Victorian Classic Revival style.

YOU CAN'T BUY YOUR WAY INTO AN
UNTOURIST GUIDE BOOK
We take no advertising or payment of any kind.
Recommendations that make it into Untourist guide books
are earned by merit only. It's nice to know that
there are some things money can't buy,

THE HERITAGE
On the Botanic Gardens
Edward Street Brisbane Q 4000
$$$$
Tel 3221 1999
Fax 3221 6895
Tollfree reservations 1800 773 700

Of the European style hotels (see Hotels, traditional above) in Australia, The Heritage in Brisbane is one the best. In fact we have given it our very highest rating because it has the best of everything. It has already become to Brisbane what the Hotel Windsor is to Melbourne – it characterises its city perfectly: the Windsor Melbourne's, reserved, interior and traditional way of doing things and The Heritage the fresh, open and cheerful sub-tropical demeanour of the new Brisbane. The Heritage tends to be where visiting celebrities stay – Pavarotti, Prince, Tina Turner, Madonna, Michael Bolton, etc.

The Heritage has a combination of conveniences and attributes that are fairly exceptional, even for a top hotel. It is in a prime position, with all rooms overlooking one of the most beautiful stretches of the Brisbane River. The Brisbane Botanic Gardens are adjacent and it's only a few minutes walk to the heart of the business and shopping district. The Brassiere on The River, with its large, comfortable cane furniture and umbrellaed courtyard, is perfect for breakfast and alfresco dining.

The Heritage was developed around the old Port Office precinct, which recalls the importance of the early Port of Brisbane. Completed in 1880, the Port Office is of Victorian Classic Revival style, including detail associated with Italianate Palazzo architecture

In the redevelopment, some extensions post-dating the 1880 Port Office were demolished and the original dignity of the

German born-and-bred Holger Hirle, a music enthusiast, is General Manager

streetscape is retained with the close neighbours the Naval Offices, Smellies Warehouse and the Port Office Hotel (formerly the Shamrock). Inside, the building has been adapted for shops and, on the upper floor, a fine restaurant (Siggis – see 10 PLACES TO EAT). Contemporary additions include the heated outdoor swimming pool, Health Centre, Grand Ballroom and function rooms, business amenities and the main hotel structure.

The informal Pavilion Bar and courtyard is a popular Brisbane meeting spot on Friday nights and The Heritage enjoys a strong local patronage.

Gentle service and fresh flowers mark your arrival, the decor is understated and concentrates more on works of art rather than overt glitz. The restaurants are all good.

"Sounds laughable, perhaps, to someone from, say, Melbourne, but we like to be here because of the music. We go to every concert we can. [The Heritage Hotel sponsors The Australian Chamber Orchestra] I'm full of admiration for the new **Queensland Conservatorium** *on the South Bank. Its concert hall, from an acoustic point of view, is outstanding. There are panels you can move out or make flush to the wall – for chamber music they can be angled differently. Facilities for students are incredible with 50 rooms, totally soundproofed – there can be a tromboneist in one room, drummer in the next and yet not hear each other."*

Holger Hirle

INN ON THE PARK
$$$

507 Coronation Drive,
Toowong, 4066
Tel 3870 9222
Fax 3870 224

This self-styled inn, one of the few in Brisbane, would be at the very top of our recommendations if it had just a little bit more personal style in its decor. Despite that, Inn on the Park lives up to its slogan, "The only thing we overlook is the River", and we highly recommend it – particularly if you have a car. (It's only a few minutes out of the centre of Brisbane and parking is easy.) Not so easy, however is actually finding it. The approach from Coronation Drive is easy, but actually finding your way to the door is a challenge. Overlooking the south reaches of Brisbane and shaded by giant palms, jacaranda and umbrella trees. Has self-contained apartments in addition to good sized traditional rooms – great for a longer stay, a laundry and ironing room, a small pool, a surprisingly good restaurant and room service if you prefer it. Ask about the Executive Ladies Package (if you are a lady) and the Gourmet Sunday Brunch (if you are a gourmet and there on Sunday).

CONRAD TREASURY
$$$$

William and George Streets
Brisbane Q 4000
Tel 3306 8888
Fax 3306 8880

In the early days, major Brisbane construction was in timber and in 1864, a great fire destroyed many of the city's finest buildings. Then came the gung-ho developers who quickly despatched most of what was left. Fortunately an international hotel chain perceived value in retaining Brisbane's old Treasury and former Lands Administration buildings and created The Treasury Hotel Casino. The idea that casinos contribute to an environment, however, or even provide a worthwhile experience, does not fit comfortably with untourism. The ability to pick up a good mid-week deal on accommodation, or perhaps an interest in historic buildings may persuade you to try the Treasury (the hotel and casino are in separate buildings).

The turn-of-the-century hotel color scheme and leather-dominated decor are true to tradition, if a little fusty. No swimming pool or health club. Special rates and packages available outside the weekend and special events times.

APARTMENT HOTELS

Brisbane and the Gold Coast were the first places in Australia to develop the hotel apartment concept whereby apartments are strata titled and owned by individuals who agree to "pool" them for hotel use. Many of the apartments in the same building do not belong to the hotel pool, but remain in private use. Self-contained and often styled with interior details that appeal to private ownership (that is, they are less likely to have the stamped-out look of many hotels), the best provide generous, comfortable and good-value accommodation. In addition there is 24-hour reception, a service system and easy access to provisions or take-away food.

CENTRAL BRUNSWICK
$$/$$$

455 Brunswick Street
Fortitude Valley, Brisbane Q 4006
Tel 3852 1411   Fax 3852 1015

This recent addition to Brisbane qualifies

for mention on the grounds of value-for-money, staff friendliness and because of its location in an area bustling with new restaurants, cafes and shops. Building style and decor are very ordinary, but all the basic facilities are there, including a spa, sauna gynnasium. The rooms have plenty of natural light. Loft,studio and one bedroom apartments.

DOCKSIDE
$$$/$$$$

44 Ferry Street, Kangaroo Point, Q 4169
Tel (07) 3891 6644
Fax (07) 3891 6900

In years to come there will probably be many places like the Dockside in Brisbane

but right now it is hard to find good accommodation right on the River. Staying at the Dockside you can enjoy that special experience of strolling down to your own jetty and catching the ferry along the Brisbane River to the centre of the city.

(Dockside cont'd)

Being on the ferry run means you have easy access to most places in Brisbane from the South Bank Arts complex to the markets at Eagle Street Pier. Tariff includes full buffet breakfast.

The Dockside complex takes up a large slice of Kangaroo Point and consists of the apartment hotel, private apartments, convenience shopping (general store, newsagent, etc) a pool, gym, a marina and several restaurants – none of which actually make it into our "best in Brisbane" list but they are certainly handy.

The apartments are spacious and fully equipped with most things you would need. It is also very easy to get extra things supplied – such as champagne flutes and essential things of that nature. The decor is as good as most luxury hotels of the Sheraton/Hilton style and we found it a perfect place to make your base in Brisbane if your stay runs over a few days.

QUAY WEST
$$$$

132 Alice Street
Brisbane Q 4000

Tel 3853 6000
Fax 3853 6060
Tollfree 1800 672 726

This well-positioned apartment hotel overlooking the Botanic Gardens(picture below) has one, two and premium two-bedroom suites. Around one third of the apartments belong to the hotel pool, the remainder being privately occupied. Each apartment has a bathroom (some have two), kitchen,laundry, living area and balcony and each has a view over the Gardens. Quay West's appeal is all the greater for the young, charming and attractive employees who add further freshness to its presentation. McMahon's restaurant has won top awards and is open

for breakfast, lunch and dinner. The recreation area has a swimming pool, spa, sauna and gymnasium. Other services include mail and courier, secretarial and multi-lingual assistance.

ROYAL ALBERT
$$$

Cnr Elizabeth and Albert Streets
Brisbane Q 4000 (opposite Myer Centre)

Tel 3291 8888
Fax 3229 7705
Tollfree 1800 655 054

Because the foyer of this convenient apartment hotel is rather small and unassuming, the first impression is that if you book in here, you'll finish up in an old office filing cabinet. Not so. Although historic Perry House was built in 1880 and spent most of its life as an office block altered and reshaped from time to time to suit tenants' needs, its transformation into an apartment hotel is very successful. The interior has been returned to 1880's style and the rooms are as comfortably spacious as the era demanded. Even "standard" rooms are quite large. The building is in the city, with all the advantages of proximity and convenience that comes with this kind of location. The light decor chosen for the interior makes an appropriate adjustment for the shadowing caused by the surrounding buildings. Each apartment has a kitchenette and laundry and there is also a conference centre. Currently, the Royal Albert has some excellent weekend specials for two-night stays. A clever piece of inner-city adaptation has made possible plenty of space for car parking – the vehicles are stacked Japanese style. The building has an outside fire escape which adds to its period charm. Down below is the tiny Cafe Mondial with a very friendly atmosphere, good food and Spanish music.

GUESTHOUSES/B&Bs
While some places call themselves B&Bs there is often a crossover point where it would be just as accurate to call the establishment a guesthouse. So we have opted for "guesthouse" to cover both types of place. Guesthouses are a fairly recent phenomenon in Queensland and many of them are excellent. As we go to press, our two favourites in Brisbane are Thornbury House and Waverley Paddington B&B. A third, Annie's Shandon Inn, has special merit for its quaintness, low cost and the fact that it's in the middle of the city. All have the following features in common: they offer an authentic experience of Brisbane living, both in architecture and in their ability to give easy access to the best the city has to offer.

ANNIE'S SHANDON INN
$$

405 Upper Edward Street
Brisbane Q 4000

Tel 3831 8684
Fax 3831 3073

Annie's is one of the quirkiest guesthouses we've ever come across. It is a quaint, brightly painted, two-storey stucco building that looks like a cartoon sketched in a forgotten plot between tall office buildings. Its homeliness is immediately established in the entrance hall – the wall is crowded with family photographs accompanied by a family history covering key events in Brisbane's history. The original Annie was born in Ireland, migrating to Brisbane in 1870. Now her grand-daughter runs the Inn. The rooms are modest, decorated in either pink or blue; some have ceiling fans and some of the iron beds have old-fashioned canopies. Washbasins are in all the rooms; only a few are en suited. On the ground floor is the common room where breakfast is served, downstairs a kitchen and laundry. The outdoor deck gives a mouse's eye view of the city buildings and this is where to catch the breeze. The area has restaurants and the city proper is only a five-minutes walk away. Rent must be paid in advance, tariff includes breakfast.

THORNBURY HOUSE
$$/$$$

1 Thornbury Street
Spring Hill
Brisbane Q 4000

Tel 3832 5985
Fax 3832 7255

A recent addition to Brisbane B&B/guesthouses, Thornbury exemplifies several features that mark it as a top stopover. It is in a traditional house of the area; it is within walking distance of the city and some of its best restaurants, and it fits like a glove into the local streetscape. With rather more rooms than the usual B&B, Thornbury would be an ideal place for a group of friends on holiday, or for corporate letting. There are five double rooms (one ensuite) and four singles. Built in 1886 for a merchant, the house has been decorated in colonial style and colours. There are three lounging areas, including the private and cool latticed front verandah with comfy armchairs. The timber-walled garden downstairs where breakfast is served is also the perfect setting for trying out some of the fine local take away food. For breakfast, fresh fruit salad comes with cereal and yoghurt and a full cooked breakfast. There are tea and plunger coffee facilities. No air conditioning, but good ceiling fans. Owner, Michelle Mullens.

WAVERLEY PADDINGTON B&B

$$/$$$

5 Latrobe Terrace
Paddington Q 4064

Tel 3369 8973
Fax 3876 6655
Mobile 0419 741 282

The inner-city suburb of Paddington is renowned for its Queenslander homes and tropical gardens. Waverley Paddington is part of this tradition. Built in 1888 in the local traditional design, which takes advantage of every passing cool breeze, Waverley has been refurbished in a warm,

colonial style with owner Annette Henry adding contemporary features like self-contained apartments and a spacious upstairs verandah that takes in city views. On the top level facing Latrobe Terrace, there are two large bedrooms with en suites, air-conditioning and television. On the same level there is also a large lounge, a dining room and kitchen. On the mid level are two self-contained apartments with private entrances. On the lower level is a large outdoor entertainment area and a garden shaded by two large mango trees. Annette, who is English born, has spent about 20 years in Australia and has travelled the country widely, using her personal homework to help shape her very fine and welcoming B&B. Tariff includes full breakfast.

WONGA VILLA
$$$

194 Bonney Avenue, Clayfield
Tel/Fax 3862 2183
Mobile 0411 551 811

This really well-renovated rambling old Queenslander (circa 1903) provides a cool, restful place to stay and it's only 10 minutes north of the centre of Brisbane. The relatively new owners Ros and John Whitely have made the most this fine old house with its big generous verandas, fireplaces, fine linen and furniture of the period . There are also a few surprises like the spa and sauna in the leafy courtyard. Wonga Villa has kitchen facilities, outside smoking only and is not suitable for children.

BACKPACKERS

Brisbane is a popular transit stop for backpackers on their way to explore the rest of Queensland and a popular base for casual work, with hostels offering all comers free work assistance. Since the opening of the Palace Backpackers, the backpacker is now probably the best catered - for traveller in Brisbane.

AUSSIE WAY Backpackers
$

34 Cricket Street
Brisbane Q 4000
Tel 3369 0711

Close to the Transit Centre (though its not simple to get to – streets in this area twist and turn and become one-way at the most inconvenient moments), Aussie Way is rather like a French pension. Established in one of Brisbane's earlier colonial homes (circa 1872), this two-storey timber house with wrought-iron lace verandahs, bullnose verandah cover and lattice front decoration is typically Queensland in building style. Here is the list of offerings: single and double dormitories; self catering and laundry facilities, security lockers, VIP and YHA discount for direct bookings, short walk to Paddo and Caxton Street; ISD phone, free work assistance, car parking, luggage storage and coffee. Only a few minutes' walk to city, GPO, restaurants, pubs, showgrounds, XXXX Brewery, swimming pool.

PALACE BACKPACKERS
$/$$

Cnr Ann & Edward Streets
Brisbane Q 4000
Tel 3211 2433 Fax 3211 2466
Tollfree for bookings 1800 676 340

The Salvation Army's People's Palace has recently been turned into one of the most

attractive and well-positioned backpacker establishments in the country. The historic landmark building is one of Brisbane's most beautiful, embraced by three wrap-around wrought-iron verandahs and cornered with a hexagonal Gothic tower. POSITION: opposite Central Railway Station; a short walk to the Transit Centre coach terminal; one block from Brisbane City Mall; within walking distance to the heart of the city.

FACILITIES: large, air-conditioned, well-equipped self-catering kitchen; disabled facilities; TV and relaxation lounges with free cable TV; coin laundries; 24-hour reception and tour and information desk; rooftop sundeck and barbecue and fine city views; Down Under Bar and Grill–open until late with great-value meals, entertainment including latest music videos, movies and major sporting events on big screens. Even dancing on the tables when the night warms up; pool tables; Palace Cafe, open for breakfast and lunch.

ACCOMMO-DATION: VIP discounts; choose between air conditioning and ceiling fans, single, twin, double and dorm rooms. FREE linen, work assistance, use of barbecue on rooftop sundeck, international newspapers.

YELLOW SUBMARINE

$

66 Quay Street
Brisbane Q 4000

Tel 3211 3424

While it's a bit tricky getting there owing to the odd angled roads, one-way streets and general busyness of the area, the Yellow Submarine (a converted 1860s, three-storey house) is very well located. It's four minutes' walk from the City and the Transit centre. Rooms available are twins, doubles and shares. There are barbecue areas, courtyards, gardens, a bush house, laundry, kitchen, dining room and TV lounge.

Below: Yellow Submarine

A thing to do in Brisbane used to be to dress up in silly costumes. Obviously beer bottle outfits were big (see front cover).

7 Things to Do

INCLUDES: The sort of things that make the savvy locals glad they live in Brisbane. Ranging from hanging off a cliff from a rope, to cheap ways to fill in a few hours when the weather's "crook".

W e've restricted this chapter to collections of things, or special experiences rather than one-offs like "go for a ride on the River". You'll find plenty of these in the area and specialty chapters. In any weather, for any age, any interest, any purse (empty or full), Brisbane has plenty of things to do, especially out-of-doors.

Here are a few more ideas:

Hanging around.

At the cliffs at Kangaroo Point on any day you can sit and watch sane men, women and children walk off the cliffs backwards, with only rope to hold them. Abseiling is a very popular pastime and the beautiful cliffs at Kangaroo Point are the place to do it. Anyone with a length of rope can go and throw themselves off, as the cliffs are prepared with anchor points every two metres, but it's not for the uninitiated and we advise that you take some serious instruction from the **Outdoor Pursuits Group** (OPG). There are many free gass barbeques and tables at the top and bottom of the cliffs where you can view daredevil antics and enjoy brilliant city views.

The misses Huie aobserve the Trail from a duck-hide.

The Boondall Wetlands Reserve Canoe Trail

North of the airport, 707 hectares of wetland was preserved in 1990 by the Brisbane City Council as well as some long corridors of wetlands within the city. Mangroves may seem just like mud and sticks, but if you enjoy this stuff, Boondall is a very fine example of managed wetlands with walking tracks, board walks, bike tracks, hides and a canoe trail. These throughways provide great ways to appreciate these areas which live within the sea's boundaries. Teeming with life, the mangroves supported and supplied many medicines and sites for ceremonies for the aboriginal tribes in the area. This is represented by the **Nurri Millen Totems**. As a result of an interesting work-skills program, Murries and Islanders have created a unique site-specific installation at Boondall. These totems are placed near a site related to a plant and animal habitat and also make connections with tools, dreaming and camp life. Such areas have been opened up by these canoe trails and at five kilometres, this is not the longest of the canoe trails. The **Bulimba Creek Trail** (*place of the magpie lark*) in East Brisbane runs for 10.3 kilometres, and the **Oxley Creek Trail** nearly 10. When visiting these trails you should take a good hat, some drinking water ("water, water everywhere and not a drop to drink"). Only enter on or leave the trail at marked access points. Happy paddling.

More details: Call BCC Parks - North.

The dilli totem by Ron Herley

Canoe the River

Another recommendation is the one-day Brisbane River canoeing trip. For around $75, you are transported from the OPG office in Sherwood (near Indooroopilly) up-stream to Fernvale where instruction begins and the trip starts. River travel is always nice but at this un-motorised level it's a joy – the wildlife, the flora, the quiet all make this quite a trip. All equipment is supplied for both these activities and a lunch is provided on the river day trip.

Up the creek with no canoe?

No problem as there are a few places hiring out canoes and appropriate equipment: **Goodtime Surf and Sail**, 29 Ipswich Road, Woolloongabba; **Rosco Canoes**, 388 Lutchwich Road, Windsor; **Wild Adventure Sportz**, 3/243 Edward Street, Brisbane.

A FavouritePlace

Boondall Wetlands is a place I especially enjoy. A rich mosaic of coastal habitats, it contains wetlands of critical importance to wading and migratory birds.

The best way to start exploring the area is from the Visitor Centre just off the Gateway Arterial Road at Boondall. Get an early start to the day, don your walking shoes, hat and sunscreen and look out for the wildlife. You might be lucky enough to spot a chestnut teal, glossy ibis or grass owl.

You can cycle the bikeway from the Boondall Roundabout to Nudgee Creek, canoe the sheltered waters of Nundah and Nudgee Beach Creeks or drop a line and catch your own dinner. Of course, there are barbecue and picnic facilities, so it is also the perfect location for a family outing. I like to walk along the sandflats at Nudgee Beach and through the mangrove forest which comes alive with birdlife.

JIM SOORLEY
Lord Mayor

QUIET INTERLUDES

Queensland Museum

The museum's galleries are divided into six well defined themes: animals, fossil animals, social history, maritime archaeology, temporary exhibitions and a reference centre.   Some of the displays: **Endangered Species** : Threatened Wildlife of Queensland. Dioramas feature preserved specimens and research stories on the processes threatening wildlife. **Animals**: Queensland is home to six of the world's seven marine turtle specie, 20 of the worlds 54 sea snake species, and the saltwater crocodile. Display focuses on the life history and conservation of these marine reptiles. **Whales** : The display looks at an important and dirty industry of whaling, showing the tools of the trade as well as archival films of a local whaling station. The collection contains skeletal remains of both baleen and toothed whales. **Maritime Archaeology**: On 29 August 1791, HMS Pandora, en route from Tahiti to England with 14 captured mutineers from HMS Bounty, sank in 33 metres after being holed on the Great Barrier Reef. Since 1983 the Museum has been surveying and excavating the wreck. Videos screen hourly from 10 am and run for a total of 40 minutes. South Bank Open 9.30am–5pm daily

State Library of Queensland Queensland Cultural Centre, Stanley Street, South Bank. Open Sunday to Friday, 10am–5pm (closed Saturdays and public holidays) In the same building, **The John Oxley Library** has the best collection available of Queensland history – it includes print material, photographs, art works, manuscripts, personal papers, business and other archives.

Hire a bicycle or roller blades

There are not many places to hire bikes in this city, which is funny because you see so many bikes and many tracks, Brisbane is more bike friendly than even Melbourne. There is a bicycle track book you can get from the BCC that displays all the bike tracks and their gradations. Or you could just ride around town – it's the best way to get from the city to South Bank or the city Botanic Gardens. The traffic in the city is fairly calm, there are a lot of one-way streets, which makes for easy riding. **Brisbane Bicycle Hire**, 87 Albert Street, Brisbane. For rollerblade hire, **Skate Biz,** 101 Albert Street.

Bridge to Bridge Bike Ride

Ben Wilson of the Bicycle Institute of Queensland picks this as a top ride from his book Greater Brisbane's Best Bike Rides. *Here is the early portion of it. For more detail, you'll need the book, so call BIQ.*

Take a CityCat to **Hoogley Street**, Hill End, and ride along Orleigh Street. Ride past **South Brisbane Sailing Club** and follow the bike signs along Riverside Drive. Great views sweep across the River to Toowong. Lots of places to stop and rest in the parkland. After passing beneath the **Merivale railway bridge**, there's a sign indicating the end of the bike path. Through some railings you'll find the concrete path to Kurlipa Point, passing under **William Jolly Bridge**. Good stopping point at the park with its facilities and great views. Moving onto a wide and well-marked timber boardwalk, past the State Library and across the river are the Commonwealth Law Courts. At the end of the boardwalk is **Victoria Bridge** and from here you can make the choice of following the path to South Bank with its restaurants, picnic, barbeque areas and lagoon, or go down Melbourne Street (beware of traffic) to West.

Cyclists commuting under the Riverside Expressway.

Heritage Trails

The BCC Heritage Unit has put together a set of walking trails. There are 10 walks, but some of them can also be drives. The trails are: The City (see detail 3 THE CENTRE); New Farm (south and north); Fortitude Valley; Toowong Cemetery; Brisbane Riverfront; Windsor; Hamilton; Wynnum to Manly; Latrobe and Given Terraces, Paddington. You can pick up detailed guides from the Brisbane Tourism booths at the **City Hall**, off King George Square, or in the Queen Street Mall. (Both information booths are staffed by local Brisbane experts). The **City Centre** and the **Brisbane Riverfront** trails can be combined into an excellent morning or afternoon

And, if you are interested in 1860s and 1930s Brisbane architecture, visit the Woollongabba Village section of Logan Road (detail, 5 SOUTH OF THE RIVER). This is also where you will find some of Brisbane's finest antiques stores and design studios.

The Mansions on the City Trail.

IF THE WEATHER'S CROOK
(Too hot /too wet / both)

Take your umbrella as a precaution and make this a day to look over the **University of Queensland,** using the indifferent weather to check out the cinema, the eateries and the museums – all seven of them. And if it's not raining, there are the beautiful grounds and other natural attractions of the campus.

University of Queensland, St Lucia

There are various ways to get to the university, but best is by river. Brisbane's CityCat service stops a short walk from UQ's magnificent sandstone buildings in the leafy suburb of St Lucia. Bus services from the city are frequent, and if you chose to drive, two parking buildings off Sir Fred Schonell Drive offer parking

Cat Stop.

for a few dollars a day. Meters are available at some other spots, and you can park anywhere at weekends.

Finding your way around the university is not always easy at first, and it's a good idea to pick up a campus map, available from the information booth at the roundabout on Sir Fred Schonell Drive or from Media and Information Services in the J D Story building on Chancellor's Place. However, if you arrive by CityCat, it's easy enough to just follow the large blue signs that give general directions.

The oldest and largest university in Queensland, UQ's main campus is almost a suburb within a suburb. Shops, restaurants, a theatre, cinema, museums, banks and other facilities cater to its 26,500 students, staff and the public.

There's usually something happening somewhere on campus. **Mayne Hall**, with its magnificent pipe organ, is often the venue for concerts (usually orchestral or choral). There are weekly Friday lunch-hour and occasional Sunday afternoon recitals by guest performers, music students and staff in the Zelman Cowan Building.

The aptly named **Cement Box** theatre is used by students and other groups for their productions, and for film buffs, the **Schonell Twin Cinema** is open most nights (admission $8). Session times are available on a 24-hour recorded message, Tel 3321 7690, or in the *Courier Mail's* entertainment guide.

Six of the university's seven museums are in the cloisters of the **Great Court** but access is limited, with most open only on weekdays. The **Anthropology Museum**, which mounts major exhibitions from its own collection of 25,000 artefacts from Australia, Papua New Guinea and the Pacific Islands, is open during semesters only on Tuesdays, Wednesdays and Thursdays from 11am–3pm.

Also well worth a visit is the **University Art Museum**, which has a collection of more than 1000 pieces of contemporary Australian art including big names such as Arthur

Boyd, Sidney Nolan, Tom Roberts, Brett Whiteley and Fred Williams. Open from 10am to 5pm weekdays.

The **Antiquities Museum** (9am–1pm and 2pm–5pm week days) has more than 1000 items from the Mesopotamian, Persian, Egyptian, Greek, Roman, Hittite and Etruscan civilisations, including pottery, glassware and coins.

There are also the **Geology Museum** (9am–4pm weekdays), the Physics Museum (1-2pm Tuesdays during semesters, or by appointment) and the Zoology Museum (weekdays 9am–4pm). The **Computer Museum** (weekday office hours) is a short walk from the Great Court, in the Prentice Building. Group visits to all museums must be booked.

Footsore and hungry after all that walking? Head for one of the university's many eateries. Our choice is **Wordsmiths**, the writers' cafe, located conveniently for literary types next to the University of Queensland Press offices and UQ bookshop. Here you'll get gourmet burgers, a range of snazzy sandwiches and real coffee of all types. Often the venue for book launches, Wordsmiths pays tribute to famous Australian authors (Carey, Malouf, Astley et al) in its sandstone carvings of their faces – a kind of Queensland Mount Rushmore, set off by gardens and a fountain.

The Wordsmith Cafe

For more basic sustenance, try one of the three campus refectories, the **Espresso Bar**, or the **Schonell Pizza Cafe** (26 varieties on offer).

Another great place to relax is the parkland that surrounds the university's three lakes, which abound with turtles, eels, waterbirds and other wildlife. This is a favourite spot with local families at weekends and if you're visiting in September/October, the jacarandas are stunning. Stroll through the riverside **Alumni Teaching Garden**, a small but lush pocket of rainforest with public walkways, and the **Una Prentice Memorial Garden**, named for the university's first woman law graduate.

A reminder, the CityCats are one of the best super-cool entertainments on offer in Brisbane. They cost only a few dollars, and will take you everywhere. A CityCat in local language is a high-speed million dollar catamaran ferry seating 138 and is the most scenic, refreshing and often the fastest way to get around the city.

The Small Art Galleries of Brisbane

In the Valley is **The Art Circuit**, 17 art galleries (private) on the **Hail and Ride** bus route that run every 15 minutes. If you don't like what you find, then there is not much of a wait. You can hop on and off the bus and browse over works from traditional paintings and woodblock prints to funky modern canvasses, elegant sculpture and delicate glassware. The ticket costs a few dollars and tours run daily through The Valley and adjacent suburbs of New Farm and Newstead. **Fire-Works Gallery** in The Valley exhibits explosively coloured fabric (Desert Designs); limited-edition screen prints and hand-tufted pure wool rugs and clothing. The bus-stops along the route have directions to locate each gallery and the route passes the River at New Farm Park to connect with the CityCats. Brunswick Street station is the closest train station to the route. This doesn't cover all the Brisbane galleries, but a good bunch are represented. Buses run between 7am–7pm but you'll have to work it around gallery hours (see below). A day ride ticket can be bought from the driver. Information on Trans Info line: 13 12 30.

The Circuit: Valley, New Farm, Newstead: **Fire-Works Gallery**, 678 Ann, Tues-Sat 11am–6pm; **Institute of Modern Art**, 608 Ann, Tues–Fri 11am–5pm; **Gilchrist Galleries**, 482 Brunswick, Wed–Sun 11am–6pm; **Jan Murphy Gallery**, Level 1, 482 Brunswick, Tues–Fri 11am–6pm, Sat 10am–5pm; **Gallery 482**, 482 Brunswick, Tues–Sat 10am–5pm; **Boab**, 486 Brunswick, Tues–Sat 10am–5pm, Sun 12–4 pm; **Philip Bacon Galleries**, 2 Arthur, Tues–Sat 10am–5pm; **Fusions Gallery**, Cnr Brunswick & Malt, Tues–Sat 11am–5pm; **New Farm Art**, 697 Brunswick, Mon–Fri 10am–7pm, Sat 10am–5pm, Sun 12–5pm; **Gallery Aesthete**, 253 Moray, Wed–Fri 10am–6pm, Sat 10am–4pm; **Milburn Gallery**, 100 Sydney, Tues–Sat 11am–5pm; **Doggett Street Studio**, 85 Doggett, Tues–Sat 12–5 pm; **Savode**, 11 Stratton, Tues–Sat 12-5.30 pm; **Fortitude Gallery**, 164C Arthur, Wed–Sat 10am–4pm; **Plotz Gallery**, 49B James, Sat 12–6pm; **Bellas Gallery**, Cnr James and Robertson, Tues-Sat 11am–6pm.

Dilli bags from Fire-Works Gallery

And for the kids ...

South Bank Butterfly House

Located a South Bank Parklands. When viewing this kind of attraction, you need to be in a calm and reflective mood. Like a library it's a quiet space and if you go for a quick look, you'll want your money back. As with all animals and children, it's pretty hard to get the little critters to perform at will. So patience is a virtue – pay and stay. The longer you stay the more you see, otherwise you might think it a bit expensive. However, there is a lot to see in a small space. It contains the world's largest collection of live Australian butterflies. Downstairs are the bugs, insect giants and spiders (the really good ones are behind bullet-proof glass). Open 8am–5pm.

Ulysses Butterfly.   *Papilio Ulysses.*

Sciencentre

The new Queensland Museum also extends its operations across the River to a most eclectic **Sciencentre** in George Street. It has an interactive display for children that intrigues them for hours, while their elders can delight in many levels of various changing displays.

Tandem bicycles

Have fun with a friend, rent a tandem bike from Double Jaunt Tandems, South Bank, on the River in front of suncorp Piazza.

FOR MORE THINGS TO DO

• Check out appropriate day trips in 13 OUT OF BRISBANE
• Go shopping, see 11 THINGS TO BUY
• Read a book, see a list of recommended Brisbane books in 11 THINGS TO BUY. For where to buy them, check out the list of great Brisbane book shops in the same chapter.
• Check 8 ARTS AND SHOWS for more ideas
• Have a long, delicious meal, see 10 EAT AND DRINK
• Get **Serious Persuits** to customise a tour for you. Suggested areas of interest: architecture, the arts, leisure and sport, regional food and wine. Angela Ramsay, 99 Cubberla Street, Fig Tree Pocket, Q 4069.

The first performers in the Cremorne theatre in Brisbane – they ke

eir day jobs.

8 Arts and Show

INCLUDES Mrs Croft's obscene act; David Malouf – a writer's town; Matilda's portentous wink and nod; getting the most from the South Bank; Murri art and the Kooemba Jdarra theatre; the major Arts performers and the fringes theatres; Brisbane rock, jazz; the best galleries; film and cinemas.

Croft's Amphitheatre appears to be credited with the honour of being Brisbane's first entertainment space. Built south of the River, not far from the current Arts complex, it was run by Mr Croft with occasional and rather alarming appearances by Mrs Croft on the high wire. The following review of one of the good lady's acts appeared in the *Moreton Bay Courier* in 1847:

On Tuesday evening, the amusements at Mr Croft's theatre were varied by the appearance of Mrs Croft on the tightrope. Making due allowances for the timidity natural to a first performance, she acquitted herself tolerably. The recitation on Law was sufficiently amusing, for the learned lecturer's mock Latin was quite equal to English. We looked in vain, however, for the deeds of daring so modestly announced by Mr Croft; the most daring deed of the evening was the introduction of an obscene song, an outrage without precedent in our experience of public amusements. That the song was encored by part of the audience could be no excuse for the insult offered to the rest; nor could any circumstance justify the unsolicited repetition of the indecency at a later period of the evening. That Mr Croft selected this song to grace the first appearance of his wife may perhaps demonstrate his own notions of propriety, but he will find it dangerous to measure public opinion by such a standard. We would advise him not to suffer such gross impropriety in future.

It must be noted that Croft's "obscene song" and "the indecency at a later period of the evening" would probably have been more at home in the rough and rude environment of the South Bank of Brisbane in 1847 than the rather pompous reviewer. Rough-and-tumble Mr Croft's Theatre was followed by more formal and legitimate entertainment houses, such as the Cremorne, the Bohemia, the Tivoli, Her Majesty's and, in 1888, the grand Opera House in Queen Street, which had a seating capacity of 2700 - more than any current house anywhere in Australia, including the Sydney Opera House and the Melbourne Arts Complex. The stories of entertainment in Brisbane in those early days are an entertainment in themselves.

PLENTY OF FINE WRITERS

Scratch most Queenslanders and you'll find a writer. The significance of writing and writers here is not broadly recognised outside literary circles, but a glance at a list of Queensland authors, the number of quality book shops in Brisbane and the titles published through houses such as Queensland University Press, is testimony to the claim that Brisbane is a writer's town and Queensland is a writer's state. Ex-pat Brisbane born editor, William Frazer recalls:

Dragging on her ever-present cigarette, Thea Astley looked down the table at her dinner companions at Writers' Week during the 1992 Adelaide Festival. Someone had just pointed out that most of those at the table were Queenslanders: Thea, David Malouf,

Rodney Hall, Susan Johnson, Tony Maniaty, Tom Shapcott, Judith Rodriguez. They started ticking off names of lauded Queensland writers now living elsewhere: Jessica Anderson, Peter Porter, Gwen Harwood, Janette Turner Hospital, Hugh Lunn, Matt Condon. Thea Astley suggested the hot-house theory, something to do with the climate, but it was agreed that the most profound literary influence was the set of school books called the Queensland School Reader.

David Malouf, Brisbane-born and inter-nationally acclaimed writer, explained: *When these readers were considered, one of the things the people who put them together had in mind was that the majority of kids would be leaving school after the Scholarship year [the end of primary school] which,* at the latest would be 14 years old. The entire curriculum was laid out in the series of 12 readers. Really bright kids could get through them and do the scholarship at 12.

The idea was that regardless of when they left school, they would have been introduced to virtually the whole of English lyric poetry. There were excerpts from about 59 novels, wads of Shakespeare, Arabian Nights, Turgenev, Tolstoy, Benjamin Franklin, the Gettysburg Address. It was put together in 1906-1907, introduced around World War I and continued until 1974. Anyone who went to school in Queensland during those years, has all that literature in common. Queensland writers of all ages, scattered over the world, all shared that reading heritage in common and still do, even if they left school at 12.

TRIBUTE TO THE WORDSMITHS

The **Albert Street Literary Trail** runs from Adelaide to Alice streets past 32 bronze plaques that feature quotes from the works of major writers who have written about Brisbane.

Wordpool "Literary cabaret: *wordpool* – a new, fast-paced, funny evening designed by the Queensland Writers' Centre with readings, discussions, poetry, and improvisation by some of Austraia's best language innovators...", *The Sunday Mail*. Two six-week sessions a year. For the opportunity to hear debaters and novelists in Brisbane read out their latest works to irreverent packed audiences over pasta, oysters and wine, contact Queensland Writers' Centre for dates and location.

During **Brisbane's Writers Week**, in September, you can hear and meet local writers. For general enquiries about literature in Brisbane, The Queensland Writers' Centre is at 535 Wickham Terrace.

Bribane's foremost arts venue, the **Queensland Performing Arts Complex** is administered by the Queensland Peforming Arts Trust, produers of the Brisbane Festival and Out of the Box children's festival.

Queensland Symphony Orchestra

QSO has a 50-year tradition of touring, covering an average of 3,500 km each year and giving more than 100 performances to around 100,000 people. The Queensland Youth Symphony began in the '60s and now has 400 players in five different ensembles and three full symphony orchestras. "It is as good a youth orchestra, if not better, than I have ever played with," said Sir Yehudi Menuhin.

CHAMBER MUSIC ENSEMBLES

Brisbane's **Pehihelion** is one of Australia's premier ensembles with an unusual combination of instruments – clarinet, viola, cello and piano. Some 20 to 30 works have been specially written for them and they specialise in Australian contemporary music. **Winds of the Southern Cross** had a stunning success in its recent tour of Canada. Its repertoire is always interesting and the individual players

are among the best in their fields. An ensemble to watch – the **Griffith Trio**. There are also the **Badeinerie Players** and the **Cantiliena Singers**, a baroque acapella group of around 12. The best chamber music venue is the Conservatorium Theatre – its size (seats around 700) intimacy and accoustic value are tops.

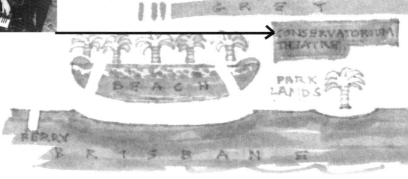

Falstaff

Opera Queensland

In addition to four major operatic productions a year in Brisbane, Opera Queensland presents smaller operatic productions, musicals, concerts and tours throughout the state, from Cairns to Gold Coast. In Brisbane, performances are in the Lyric Theatre.

Queensland Ballet

Widely regarded for its vitality, imagination and versatility, this vibrant group is also Australia's oldest professional dance company. Peformanaces in the Lyric and Cremore Theatres.

Queensland Theatre Company

Under the directorship of actor Robyn Nevin AM, this Brisbane-based company is the major drama producer in the state. Peformances are in the Cremorne Theatre.

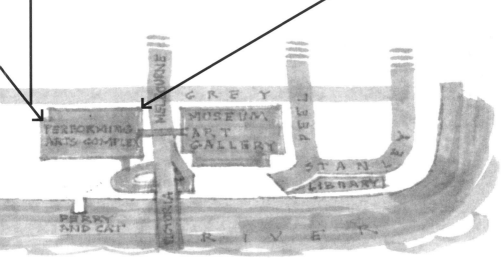

THE CULTURAL AWAKENING

The Arts emphasis probably moved from the affordable, simple art form of literature to the more complex publicly funded performing arts with the completion of the South Bank performance spaces in the 1980s. With a wink and a nod from Matilda, the 13-metre plastic kangaroo, the Arts became serious business in Brisbane and is now one of the top five industries in the state. With money and infrastructure in place, the energy was kindled which, in turn, spawned a whole host of small arts companies, highly creative performance artists and born-again venues.

Expressions

Since its foundation in 1985 by Maggi Sietsma, Expressions (pictured right) has achieved national and international recognition. "An extraordinary company... Perfectly trained virtuoso dancers... Maggi Sietsma has a unique choreographic concept and style which does not fit into any pre-existing category of modern dance." *Ballet International/*Tabz Actuell.

Expressions is a dedicated and highly talented group of professional actors who perform new classic theatre. Their repertoire has included fine performances of *Romeo and Juliet*, *The Romance of Orpheus*, *The Tale of Macbeth*, *Salome* and *Oedipus Rex*.

Using a unique blend of storytelling, circus skills, clowning, movement and magic, **Anna Yen's** (pictued left) one-woman show, "Chinese Take Away", wends its way from old China to modern Australia, passing through Hong Kong in the '30s, suburban Sydney in the '60s, uncovering hidden heroines, real and imagined, who resist enslavement from poverty, racism and dislocation.

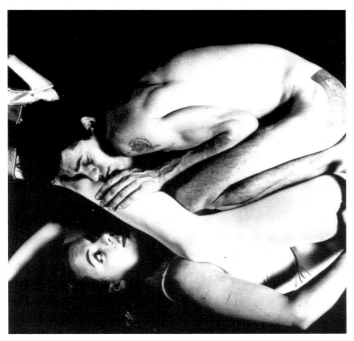

Rock 'n' Roll Circus

Incorporating live music and physical feats in everything from major works to performances for festivals, street fairs and corporate events, Circus can produce a five-minute spot or a full evening of entertainment. "Erotic, perverse, enigmatic, sadistic, sentimental, street-smart, funny, surreal and is altogether terrific," said *The Australian*.

Elision Ensemble

Australian new music performance. Innovative projects include contemporary opera, site-specific installations, improvisation and electronic music, plus an extensive repertoire combining instruments from Western and Asian traditions.

Bev Langford in The Shoe-Horn Sonata, La Boite.

La Boite

Contemporary theatre at its most interesting can be found at La Boite near Lang Park. Encouragement for Queensland artists is the hallmark of this small, dynamic company. Established on a tradition of innovative and challenging approaches, La Boite has captivated audiences with its adventurous programm-ing and artistic excellence.

MURRI ARTS

Queensland is home to Australia's largest population of Aboriginal and Torres Strait Islanders, and Brisbane often hosts the many fine Murri and Torres Strait Islander groups from the rest of the state.

Kooemba Jdarra is not the Queensland Theatre Company with black faces. For these Aboriginal people, their relationship to the theatre is something quite different, a difference that can be seen and felt during their performances.

The Kooemba Jdarra Aboriginal Corporation, Australia's leading Aboriginal and Torres Strait Islander theatre company is based at Metro Arts, the home they share with a number of arts groups. The building has had quite a colourful history. A sandstone structure, it has stood in the centre of Brisbane since 1880. It lay dormant for many years, and then became the federal government narcotics headquarters. "Strange, considering the amount of heads working in the place now!" comments Lafe Charlton, Artistic Director of Kooemba Jdarra.

After 20 years, Metro is now a thriving arts hive with a number of art organs pumping out creativity from many cracks and crannies of the old building. Some of this creative output makes its way around the country and, in the case of Kooemba Jdarra, to the other side of the world. Kooemba Jdarra maintains a commitment to professionalism and excellence in the arts and is dedicated to the empowerment and self-determination of Aboriginal and Torres Strait Islander communities through the work of its performers.

The Indigenous Theatre Company is now in its sixth year of operation and aims to be around for many more years in the future. It has made inroads into the mainstream arts in Australia, which says a great deal for its standards. Splinters of black theatre are starting to happen but, generally, indigenous theatre in this country is still very much in the development stage. There are only two full-time indigenous theatre companies in operation, and both are on opposite sides of the country (Brisbane and Perth).

As the new artistic director of Kooemba Jdarra, I will continue to build on its momentum by producing works that reflect the ideas and philosophies of indigenous culture, both on traditional and contemporary levels, not only as a source of entertainment, but also as a portal of political and social change.

Lafe Charlton, Artistic Director.

Kooemba Jdarra is based in Brisbane in the Metro Arts building, 109 Edwards Street.

The best of Murri painting, carving, weapons and craftwork can be found at the Queensland Art Gallery and **Fire-Works Gallery** – "Aboriginal Art and other Burning issues" the latter is in Fortitude Valley.

Although this discerning Gallery is a commercial concern, it offers support to artists in more ways than just showing works of art. The mere existence of a credible and creative organisation that works as a commercial gallery without scrumming to the boomerang school of souvenirs must give much hope to indigenous artists.

*Marana shield design–
Joanne Currie*

The National Gallery would be proud of the standard of the work the gallery displays. The Campfire Group began as an artists' collective and, after five years, in 1995, they set up the gallery to support the art and to provide a base in the city. They have established a network of Bush Studios in and around southeast Queensland for art production, workshops and cultural exchange. We have seen a few indigenous outlets and this is one of the groups that puts their art before the tourist dollars.

Laurie Nilsen

There are monthly feature exhibitions that pit new and up-coming artists with their more exposed peers. There is always something to buy, from original postcards to major works of sculpture or painting, and there's a consultancy service for the more serious collector seeking particular works or work from remote areas.

Fire-Works – out back

678 Ann Street, Fortitude Valley, 11am to 6pm Tuesday to Saturday, 12pm to 4pm Sunday. Closed Monday.

See a more detailed description of this great gallery in 11 BEST THINGS TO BUY.

Queensland Art Gallery

One tip - the Gallery is perfect for escaping the heat in summer. With the temperature set at 22 degrees to protect the art works, there is instantly cooling. Take a free guided tour. The Gallery Shop is good for finding untourist souvenirs.

Have you heard the one about the artworks that fell off the back of a truck? Well, on one occasion, a young couple brought a selection of Papunya boards to the Gallery in the boot of a car. The curator inspected them in the car park, and three of these beautiful boards are now in the collection.

A key piece to watch out for in the Queensland Art Gallery is a series of 18 panels by Utopia artist, the late Emily Kame Kngwarreye. Emily Kame Kngwarreye died on 2 September 1996 (the artist's full name is used with permission from the Utopia community.) These Utopia panels were commissioned by the Gallery in the lead-up to a major national touring exhibition of Kngwarreye's work held in 1998, and were considered by the artist to be her contribution to the exhibition.

One of Australia's greatest contemporary artists, Kngwarreye had a very distinctive style, quite different from those of other desert artists. With their bold and captivating gestural stripes, the Utopia panels will surprise those who think that desert art is restricted to the "dot and circle school". Look closely and you'll also see dog paw prints on some panels, as the artist painted on the ground.

The collection is particularly strong on Australian contemporary art, indigenous Australian art and contemporary Asian art. In fact, the Gallery's collection of contemporary Asian art is probably the best public collection in the world.Open daily, 10am–5pm. Entry to the Queensland Art Gallery is free, except for special exhibitions. Melbourne Street, South Brisbane.

The Mangrove Monster No.2 1986 by William Yaxley

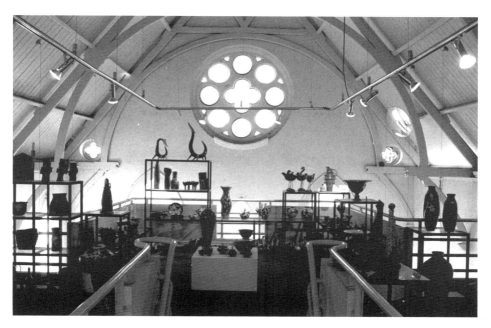

Fusions Gallery –Brisbane's first church of ceramics.

THE ART GALLERIES

Fusions Gallery, home of the Queensland Potters' Association, is the home of the best ceramics in Brisbane. The pottery and glass collections particularly are worth a visit. An excellent monthly newsletter gives all the latest in the craft and can be acquired through the gallery. Cnr Malt and Brunswick streets, Fortitude Valley.

Take a look at the latest edition of the *Brisbane Innercity Galleries Guide*, available from information centres, the Queensland Art Gallery, Queensland Museum and most city galleries. This handy publication is updated annually and provides a map and short description of the 100 or so public, commercial and artist-run gallery spaces within a 10-minute walk of the CBD.

Bellas Gallery displays leading contemporary artworks in a sophisticated fashion. Try and catch one of their eye-opening nights. 49 James Street, Fortitude Valley.

Philip Bacon Galleries leads the state in dealing in fine art in general. Exhibition openings are monthly social events starring major national and international artists, including jewellers, potters and sculptors, as well as painters. Tuesday to Saturday, 10am to 5pm. 2 Arthur Street, Fortitude Valley.

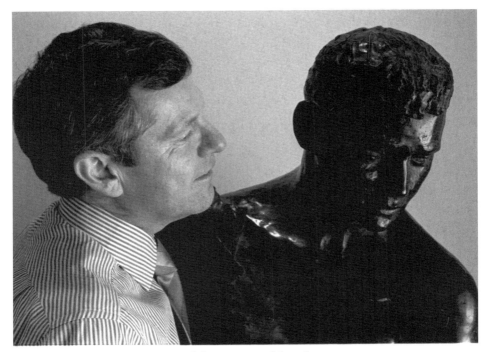

Philip Bacon and friend.

Just around the corner from Philip Bacon Galleries is a huddle of three quality galleries. The new red brick shopping centre opposite offers good dining on all levels if you need a pitstop between shopping and looking at art pieces.

Gallery 482 - modern art, Brunswick Street, Fortitude Valley.

Gilchrist Galleries, 482 Brunswick Street, Fortitude Valley.

Jan Murphy Gallery, 482 Brunswick Street, Fortitude Valley..

New Farm Art Gallery mostly specialises in drawings and paintings, with occasional artefacts and ceramics, 697 Brunswick Street, New Farm.

Milburn Gallery. Michael Milburn covers the fine-art spectrum in a long-established business, 100 Sydney Street, New Farm.

Riverhouse Galleries is known for its traditional fine arts, mostly quality Australian works, 1 Oxlade Drive, New Farm.

Doggett St Studio is an experimental area for working artists who run this space Regular exhibitions involving three artists at a time are a statement in themselves. Doggett Street, Fortitude Valley,

Institute of Modern Art is much loved by the avant garde and has frequently changing exhibitions that stimulate, enrage and amuse, 608 Ann Street, Fortitude Valley.

Away from art gallery Valley and on the other side of town are **Grahame Galleries and First Editions**, Serious collectors will like this spot not far from the thriving little village of Rosalie, 1 Fernberg Road, Milton.

Brisbane Gigs and Bands

In the 1950s, just out of Brisbane in Nudgee Beach, the young and impressionable Gibb boys started their rise to mega-stardom. They took on the initials of a local radio star of the day, Bill Gates (no relation to the Microsoft guru). The Bee Gees left Nudgee Beach behind for an unbelievable career, ultimately singing meaningless song in very high voices. Brisbane now features more than ever with the ubiquitous Savage Garden all over the world and at home the mellow tones of Powder Finger, Custard being a bit silly and Regurgitator getting all the attention with their simple, cleverly crafted songs.

Mind you, you'll be lucky to see any of these Brisbane bands in Brisbane, but you will see the next generation at some of the local gigs. Costa Zulio of JJJ in Brisbane says that the **Roxy** is his big gig choice - it's where you'll see some of the touring acts that don't fit into the mega-band class.

Mother and son, Quan and Lien Yeomans. Lien runs The Green Papaya, see 10 EAT AND DRINK

Quan Yeomans from Regurgitator doesn't like playing these places any more. He opts for the smaller spots, such as Costa's favourite, the **Zoo** run by C and Joc, who had trouble starting up again after they were closed down for building and safety reasons. An army of fans, including some of the bands mentioned above, got together to raise the funds required. They sold sponsorship plaques for the steps for $150 each - the top step was bought by Spider Bait, one of the bands that C let sleep on the floor of her house when the band first started.

The street papers *Time off, Rave* and *Scene* will give you the most up-to-date info on who's playing where and if you don't know the band, just ring the place and ask what the band is like. The other two street papers to look out for are *Brother Sister* and *Queensland Pride*. These are the gay and lesbian newspapers and they also list a range of gigs. The best place would have to be a mixed hotel called

Joc in the Zoo.

Rainbow flag, denotes broad-minded hotel.

the **Wickham Hotel** on Wickham Street, Fortitude Valley. There's always something happening there. It also has a good bistro and a top restaurant, the Grape, upstairs for dining. See 10 EAT AND DRINK.

Here are some other gigs recommended by Chris and Marie from community television Briz 31's local music show, but always check the band first: Chelsea at XXX, Super deluxe above the **Empire Hotel**, and the **Tube** in Wickham Street, for techno. These three are in The Valley. In Mary Street in town is **Crash and Burn**, a smallish gig with a low roof that packs them in with good bands, very squishy.

Jazz

Greg Quigley of **Jazzworks** (See 4 THE NORTH) laments the closing of the Bass Note in 1997 as the end of the last venues dedicated to real jazz. "Slim pickings in Brizzie now," he says. But if you really need a jazz fix, try **The Healer** in Warner Street, Fortitude Valley, which has mostly blues, or the Story Bridge Hotel, Kangaroo Point, on the weekends. Full-on trad-jazz is to be heard at the **Brisbane Jazz Club**, Annie Street, Kangaroo Point (a bit of a lonely hearts club). **Ric's Cafe** in Brunswick Street and **The Hub Internet Cafe** in Margaret Street also have irregular jazz shows in a good atmosphere.

FAST FORWARD FOR FILM

Jackie McKimmie, who lives in Brisbane, is one of the best-known Queensland filmmakers (writer and director) with her features *Waiting*, *Gino* and *Australian Dream*. Jackie, who finds the Brisbane climate and the slower lifestyle conducive to writing, supplements film-making with local theatre work.

For a long time, we didn't have film and television infrastructure here and aspiring film-makers had to go south to Sydney and Melbourne. They still do, but the locals have also recently mustered their pride and are producing some local product, in spite of the nearby Gold Coast studios, which devote themselves to international film and television productions using foreign talent. Some recent local productions: Nicole McCuaig directing the hard-hitting documentary on Schoolies Week, Rage of Innocence, and Murri director Wesley Enoch's fine short Grace; Danni Rogers, directing telemovie Paperback Hero and Michelle Warner directing Mr Pumpkin's Big Night Out.

Jackie McKimmie

Film-making is a thriving industry and the government is making a large investment in it to ensure that it becomes the leading film-production state in the nation. Film buffs can also feast on the offerings of the Brisbane International Film Festival, held annually in August, the Exposure Short Film Festival, Women on Women Festival and the Brisbane International Animation Festival, which are all on the up and up.

A young Noni Hazelhurst in 'Station'.

The mighty Wes Hall spent a lot of time on the Brisbane cricket scene after the tied test, seen here intimidating some poor bloke.

8 Sport

INCLUDES: How a sport had preference over training the troops; legendary stories, cricket, football, golf, fishing and more.

The Gabba as Sacred Ground

In 1942 Pearl Harbor had fallen, the war was now on Australia's doorstep and for the first time ever, a halt was called to first-class cricket games in Brisbane. The reality of the war finally hit home.

The city's cricket ground at Woolloongabba (The Gabba) had been requisitioned by the War Office to train troops. Yet so serious was local love of this ground and cricket, that the soldiers, training to defend the country against the might of the Japanese, did not walk on the central pitch area. They were allowed on the ground only without their army boots and training was done in bare feet.

The truth is that there are many sporting enthusiasts the world over who have heard of The Gabba even if they have never heard of Brisbane itself.

A Folk Legend

Eddie Gilbert was one of the "stolen generation", a full- blood Murri who was taken from his family as a youngster in 1929 and placed under white care. He became the man who had the great Don Bradman caught for a duck and later also bowled him out. This has become the stuff of Australian folk legend.

Gilbert was bowling for Queensland. With his first ball he dismissed the number-one opener, which brought Sir Donald Bradman to the crease. The next ball knocked Bradman's bat out of his hands and the following ball had him tripping over his own feet. On the third ball The Don was out for a duck and Gilbert went into history as one of Australia's top first-class cricketers. Only illness prevented him playing for Australia against the English bodyline tactics in 1932-33. He later played for Queensland against the West Indies, England and South Africa. Tragically, Eddie Gilbert spent his final 30 years in a psychiatric institution.

Eddie Gilbert celebrates getting Bradman for a duck on the third ball. Inset: The second ball.

The famous "down wicket, no umpire shot" as described in pubs all around the world.

A Famous Tied Test

In December 1960, the cricketing world stood still and watched The Gabba. A test was being played between Richie Benaud's Australian XI and Frank Worrell's West Indies XI. In the first innings, Garfield Sobers and Frank Worrel played, as Norman May says, "The best cricket I ever watched." Alan McGilvray said: "It was the greatest innings by the greatest batsmen." These two where merciless , scoring 100 runs in 90 minutes, and the Windies went on to score the highest West Indies score in Australia.

At the beginning of the last session of the last day (day five) with 123 runs to get and no recognised batsmen left, Richie Benaud said to Alan Davidson in a mid-pitch meeting, "Lets give it a go!" How these bowlers batted, but within sight of the last over, the wheels started to come off the Australian innings. Two balls to go after five days' intense cricket and a wicket fell, the scores were level and Australia had one wicket left. Lindsay Kline, another bowler who didn't think he would have to bat, couldn't find his batting gloves because he was sitting on them. When he walked past Frank Worrel, Frank said: "You look a little pale Lindsay." He recalls that it seemed to take forever for Wes Hall to run in to bowl. The ball finally came and Lindsay Kline played it deftly (for a number eleven) off to square leg, hesitated and then took off. Joe Solomon picked up and threw towards the stumps with Ian Meckiff sliding face down, stretching his bat toward the crease and Meckiff was run out. It was a tie, a result that was a first.

A Ticker-tape Parade

Allan Border (a legendary captain of the Australian XI), guided his home state of Queensland at The Gabba in 1995 to win the Sheffield Shield (right), the most coveted prize in Australian interstate rivalry. After trying for 67 years the Bulls had finally won by an innings and 101 runs. They made front pages all over the country and the reward was a ticker- tape parade through the Queen Street Mall. The players became Brisbane legends overnight.

The Shield competition. the only true national competition played in Australia, is envied by the rest of the world and is recognised as the best training ground possible for young cricketers. The selectors of the Australian XI cast their eyes on all the Shield sides to ensure the best possible team is chosen to whip the Poms (and the rest).

Bullets, Bulls, Broncos, Bandits, Reds, Rockets, Lions and Marrons – Brisbane sports teams all, but which ones really stand out probably depends on the game you follow.

Rugby League and Union are very popular with Australian Rules working up a lather on the sidelines. While cricket may be tops, the only event that stops Brisbane – and most of the east coast of Australia – is the State of Origin rugby league series, NSW vs Qld.

Rugby League

Ever since 1988 and the beginning of the Brisbane Bronco's Rugby League team, it's hard to find anything else to follow on the radio or TV. The current League legend would have to be Alfie Langer, or Deborah Kerr as he is referred to by those intrepid reporters H G Nelson and Rampaging Roy Slaven. Explanation? The previous bigwig, The King, as he was known, was Wally Lewis, a name to inspire fear in NSW folk.

Before the Broncos, in Rugby League terms, there was only the State of Origin match to get your dose of Mexican*-bashing, and this is where The King would weave his magic. Eventually, a young halfback came along with skills to match, or at least complement The King, who played just behind the halfback in the back line. They would dummy, show the ball and dance their way into our hearts and across the try line. Get it now? The King and I, which starred Deborah Kerr as the "I".

The Broncos surely must be the most successful team of any sport to come out of Brisbane. Just to make sure that any stray Mexicans knew where they were, a larger-than-life brass statue of The King (right) was commissioned to be placed outside The Cauldron (alias Lang Park), the then home of all Queensland State of Origin games. The Origin games started as a counter measure to the loss of Queensland players to the well bank-rolled southern teams, and also to develop talent for international test teams. The first game was in 1980 and the Queensland team included Mal Meninga, Wally Lewis and Artie Beetson...my God, no wonder they won the violent encounter. Most of the media accounts of the game gave more space to the descriptions of the upper cuts and right crosses than the play of the ball. These games, in our humble opinion, were the most fiercely contested professional sporting contests in the world. Yes, The World.

*In Queensland, anyone who lives south of Tweed Heads (on the NSW border) is known as a Mexican.

Australian Football League

The AFL is a national competition (though not as representative of the other states as Victoria). The only problem is that we have to play only other Australians as nobody else plays the silly game – more fool them. Aussie Rules is fast and hard at worst and positively invigorating at best. The Lions (previously the Bears) carry our torch for Brisbane here. Brisbane has embraced this game and as a one-team town the Bears have lots of support. They took their final form out of wreckage of the Fitzroy Club, then moved to the Gold Coast by Christopher Skase (a failed and now fugitive entrepreneur) and the next six years could only be described as hibernation. In 1993 the Bears came home to a Gabba that was undergoing a massive renovation with lights and seating for more than 23,000. That first year was not the best but it picked up in 1994. One of the big problems is that until 1990 this game was called VFL (Victorian Football League), which is a pretty ugly thing when you come from up here.

If you are ready, go throw yourself off the cliffs at Kangaroo Point. If you are not we suggest that you take some instruction from professionals. There are all sorts of adventure sports and cliffs to abseil off, mountains to climb, rapid rivers and canyons to get lost in, see 7 THINGS TO DO.

You have to get up early to catch the rowers.

Other sports

There is, it may surprise you to learn, more to Brisbane sport than cricket and football. There are 55 golf courses, two race courses, four greyhound tracks, two trotting courses, thousands of sporting clubs and grounds, and fishing ...oh boy is there fishing. Adventure sports are also very popular. There is a number of adventure sports groups that specialise in controlled recklessness: abseiling, rock climbing, white-water rafting, shark dives and many more life-threatening activities for thrill-seekers of all ages. The BCC runs activities under the banners of G.O.L.D. (growing old and living dangerously) and Chill Out at the other age end of the market.

Morning activities at South Bank.

Find the loo

The Stadium

In 1904 Australia sent a team to the St Louis Olympics which, for the first time, included boxing. We didn't win any gold medals in any sport, but boxing was pushed to a new height of popularity. On the corner of Albert and Charlotte streets where the comparatively elegant Festival Hall now stands, there used to stand a square structure with no roof and a wire fence that separated the patrons with seats and the ones who had standing room only. It also protected the better-heeled patrons from flying bottles and cans and other thrown objects.

The Stadium was packed on any given night. By 1958 it had a roof and we're sure there was a lavatory in there somewhere, but it always remained little more than a corral. Toward the end of its lifetime other activities and shows were put on, including vaudeville, wood-chopping contests and concerts of all types.

The highlight of the Stadium's history was a fight in 1916, the year before the fabled boxer Les Darcy's death in the USA of, they say, a broken heart. Darcy arrived in Brisbane by sea, travelling down the River to the city to much fanfare and a welcome by the mayor. The Stadium's low point was a riot after the towel was thrown in at a fight involving Archie (The Gympie Tiger) Bradley and Leo Darton. The crowd tore the place apart. The police were called in and no doubt inflamed the situation by using truncheons. The last fights in 1957 were poorly attended and the Stadium was demolished the next year.

Rugby Union

With all arena sports, pre-match entertainment is always a sore point with organisers, spectators and in the case of one infamous QRL grand final, the players too. The entertainment was going ahead as programmed except for the sky divers who didn't show up (or down in this case) until the game had been under way for over ten minutes and then they landed in the middle of the field. It was determined that this was no advantage to either side, so the game went on regardless.

The world famous Ballymore ground at Herston – connected to the Brisbane by Breakfast Creek – is home to the Queensland Reds, one of the top sides in the Super 12 Rugby Union series. The Reds play the best provincial teams from New Zealand and South Africa at the ground between March and June and feature some of the world's leading players in Wallaby (the Australian 13) captain John Eales, Tim Horan, Jason Little and Ben Tune.

John Eales pulling points out of the air

On two occasions at Ballymore in 1998, Wallaby captain John Eales has soared into the air to knock down penalty kicks as they were going over the cross bar. It is a feat virtually unheard of on rugby grounds around the world, and further evidence that Eales is a player of extraordinary talent. In years to come rugby fans in the bars around the ground will recall Eales's amazing performances.

Ballymore has also been the scene of some memorable tests and each year hosts matches between Australia's Wallabies and top international sides. The Rugby Union Premiership is contested each year, with matches around Brisbane, culminating in a grand final at Ballymore in September.

Eagle Farm Race Course

Horse racing in Queensland has a longer history than any other sport, dating back to 1843 – and the state's oldest official racing document is the land grant approval for Eagle Farm, now one of the premier racecourses in Australia.

On the first race day in August 1865, Brisbane was still very much a country town. Owners of horses had to be reassured that "there is no danger whatever to be apprehended from the stump holes, all of which have been received the due amount of attention required to make them firm". Spectators were transported by steamers from Brisbane to Hamilton Wharf opposite the Hamilton Hotel "whence to the course is a pleasant walk of about three quarters of a mile through the bush".

Perhaps Eagle Farm's greatest claim to fame is that the great dappled grey stallion Gunsynd ran his first race there on 11 October, 1969. Owned by a bunch of average blokes from the Queensland town of Goodiwindi, he was bought for $1300 and went on to win better than 50 per cent of his races. Gunsynd had a remarkable trait of playing to the public – his ears pricked up when the course announcer called his name and when the crowd applauded he turned to look at the grandstand. Poems and songs were written about him and he was featured on everything from tea towels to shirts. When he died in retirement in Goondiwindi, the whole town held a wake for him at the local pub.

One of Australia's greatest contemporary racing controversies took place at Eagle Farm. On August 8, 1984 a ring-in horse was substituted for an indifferent performer called Fine Cotton and the Commerce Novice was won in a thrilling finish, the winner having been backed from 33-1 to 3-1. The horse was disqualified, but all bets stood and $1 million was lost in an Australia wide betting plunge.

Of the several significant non-racing historic moments that took place at Eagle Farm, the most important took place in March 1928 when Bundaberg-born Bert Hinkler landed there after his spic solo flight from London to Australia.

The pool at Eagle Farm, fancy a dip?.....Equine only.

Golf

With Brisbane's beautiful climate it's not too hard to grow grass, but it's turning grass into a course that's the thing. There are 55 golf courses in Brisbane – that's plenty of grass. One of the better public courses is the **St Lucia Golf Links** seven kilometres from the city on Cnr Indooroopilly Road and Carawa Street Indooroopilly. The course is split by the sandy creek, and any water running though a golf course adds to its beauty and its difficulty factor. The ferry doesn't go all the way to the links, which is a shame, because the River is alway a nice way to travel on a slow day.

Very close to this course is the **Indooroopilly Golf Club**. Now this is a ripper, again close to town. Two 18-hole courses, each 72 par. On the point called Long Pocket, the eastern course has some beautiful holes but the western course is the gem. Open to the public every day except Saturday, Meiers Road Indooroopilly. Just across the river in Yeerongpilly is **The Brisbane Golf Course** – another top-rated course – one of the best in fact. The public course is only nine holes, and obviously has less to offer, but you can go around all day for around a few dollars. The pro course built in 1904, is the oldest course in Brisbane, and if you can get in, you can pay around $50 and have a run-around this smashing course, Tennyson Memorial Avenue, Yeerongpilly. The very best course in Brisbane is the **Royal Queensland Golf Club**, on the River, under the Gateway Bridge, about 20 mins from city. The course was designed by Ross Watson who also did the Indooroopilly course. Only one course and private. If you are a current member of a club and you have your membership card you will get a game if there is one to be had, West Curtin Avenue, Eagle Farm.

Golf is big in Brizzie – note the concentration of the boy in red.

Fishing near the mouth of the Brisbane River.

Fishing

"Just drop a line in anywhere, you'll catch something," said the old bloke standing in his shorts in the waist-high water of the Schulz canal near the mouth of the Brisbane River. From before sunrise the little boats start to arrive in areas like this and don't stop till late in the day.

"The fishing's good around here – the best I reckon," the lady at the bait shop in Manly told us. You will hear this story up and down the coast, in every bait shop, and at every bay, beach and stocked dam. Of course its prohibited to fish off the Brisbane River bridges, but you can throw a line in at Newstead Park or the east side of the Captain John Bourke Park under the Story Bridge. There was an older woman who spoke very little English. She was using a hand line on the Brisbane River, at the Hamilton reach and already had a bucket full of flathead. She got across that she tried to come every day but her husband wouldn't.

There are many spots that regularly attract plenty of anglers. Moreton Bay is a haven with wetlands and mangroves busily breeding fish to fill the bay. You'll find bream, whiting, tailor, snapper, flathead and the occasional mackerel. The truth is the fishing is good where you last caught them – which is just about anywhere up here.

Here are two untourist top spots:
• At the top of the Pumicestone Passage, behind Bribie Island is Caloundra, where plenty of fish pass through the narrow mouth of the passage.

• Jumpinpin is a special spot, a series

Ready to go from the Scarborough boat harbour.

of mangrove islands and narrow passages wedged between the Stradbroke islands. It's legendary – regulars say it is the best bream fishing grounds in the nation. Access (you'll have to hire a tinny) is best via Jacobs Well which has boat hire and few stores and the local Air Sea Rescue base. It also has a big boat ramp and it does get busy on the weekends. **Jacobs Well** also has a very good camping reserve which you might need if you want to really enjoy this area.

Here are a few more areas you might find worthwhile:

Hornibrook Bridge is used for nothing but fishing and ugly signage.

• Both sides of the mouth of the River, though the south side has much better access.
• Wellington Point at Waterloo Bay (south of Wynnum).
• Bramble Bay, Sandgate and Redcliffe (to the north).
• You should often find whiting around the Pine River (north), all the way up to the junction with the South Pine River. The Pine River flows into Bramble Bay, Hayes Inlet and around the Hornibrook Highway bridge – all good fishing areas.
• Moreton, North Stradbroke and Bribie islands have some of the best beach fishing on any coast. This one is hard to pick as the currents, surf and the rips make it a personal sport. The eye, the gut and a good rig make all the difference. In the colder months, from the beaches you will mostly catch mullet and tailor – otherwise it's flathead, whiting and bream.

If you intend to use any apparatus like nets or traps, we suggest that you get hold of *Guidelines for Recreational Fishing in Queensland* from the Queensland Fisheries Management Authority (QFMA). If you catch a tagged fish, don't panic. Simply telephone the QFMA to report the catch to assist with the fisheries management. Most non-reef fish have no bag limit, though size can be an issue. Here is a truncated list of legal minimum sizes: bream 23cm; flathead 30cm; perch 25-30cm; snapper 30cm; tailor 30cm and whiting 23cm.

Blue Lake Beach, North Stadbroke. Who needs to fish ?

LOCAL HERO

TAIL
(EDIBLE
BIT)
TUCKED
UNDER HERE

10 Eat and Drink

MORETON
BAY BUG
(THENUS
ORIENTALIS)
SMALL EYES
SET WIDE
APART—
UNLIKE
BALMAIN BUG
(IBACUS
PERONII)
SOUTHERN
IMPOSTER
WITH EYES
TOO CLOSE
TOGETHER

Includes: The best local produce and where to eat it; from stodge to style in 10 years; Brisbane's pioneer chefs and the very best restaurants, cafes and brasseries; the best pubs – both old and "born-again style"; Brisbane booze - both wine and beer; delis, and Ben's cheap eats.

What should you eat in Brisbane? The following description of the dinner that accompanied the 1997 Queensland wine awards might give you a few ideas. "Seafood, of course, lashings of super fresh Moreton Bay bugs and oysters, mud crabs and sand crabs, reef fish, yabbies, avocados and scallops with Buderim ginger and golden mangos from the far north. Beef tenderloins from the Darling Downs or lamb in a macadamia nut crust glazed with red wine, followed by huge prawns from the Gulf area and sweet baby crays from local waters done in chilli and garlic. The crisp sugar snap peas came from Gatton, and Warwick sent cheeses, asparagus, broad beans and Queensland blue pumpkin. Roma tomatoes appeared in basil butter. Desserts were from North Queensland and some exotic pieces of fruit went on show together with mangos and passionfruit."

Seafood, indeed, but there are a couple of basics to take on board when eating seafood in Brisbane's sub-tropical climate. The first is that most of it has been frozen, and the second is that the fishermen tell us the best of it goes south to the Sydney markets where it fetches a higher price. That's the bad news, but the good news is that, as cook extraordinaire Stephanie Alexander points out, the sort of freezing that goes on is essential because of the hot climate and that it is a special high-speed, high-temperature process that takes place on board the trawlers as the fish is caught. The result can be undetectable.

The fact that Sydney seems to snaffle the best of the catch is understandable from the fishermen's perspective because they are after the top dollar, but it doesn't do much to help Brisbane take its place as a progressive culinary centre. A bit of lobbying from the restaurant and tourist industry, and a bit of action from the state government is needed here. Why not some sort of bounty to encourage local sales of local produce?

The most famous of the local produce is the unfortunately named but most delicious, Moreton Bay Bug. Bugs are seasonal (around springtime), but out-of-season snap-frozen ones are often available. Cook them like prawns, use them as you would lobster or crayfish meat in pasta or salads, or cut them in half lengthwise and, after removing the inner gut thread, serve them warm with melted butter and lemon juice. A real treat. And for all those southerners who think Balmain Bugs are the same as Moreton Bay Bugs - they're not. The Balmain Bug, aka *Ibacus peronii* or Shovel Nose Lobster, is an imposter!

The great mud crab is, of course, the jewel in Queensland's culinary crown, but its numbers are declining as its mangrove swamp habitat becomes a hunting ground for resort developers. Sand crabs and spanner crabs are worth their space on a plate and certainly a close look - they haven't bothered to change a thing about their appearance since the Creation.

Then there's the entire Disneyland kingdom of fish: barramundi, mangrove jack and king salmon grace the tables of the eaterati everywhere, as do the gloriously sequin-scaled reef fish, much admired by informed Japanese who import our technicolor red emperors, snapper, coral trout and all the other colourful courtiers of the deep. Let's hope there will be enough left for us to enjoy in the future, as the world discovers this culinary treasure trove.

FROM STODGE TO STYLE IN TEN YEARS

Somehow, the culinary changes seem more dramatic in Brisbane than in any other Australian city, probably because it all happened so quickly and also because it was so awful before.

Like most other parts of Australia, Brisbane's eating and drinking have benefited greatly from the influence of Asian and European residents. Multicultural Brisbane's current food scene is a gastronomic gasp. There are more than 2000 licensed restaurants listed by the Brisbane City Council. The council's relaxed attitude to open-air eating has radically altered the local social scene, which has blossomed into an outdoor cafe culture. Chains of coffee shops have sprung up, providing a variety ranging from currently fashionable trends to homely old favourites. Coffee shops, bistros and wine bars have become meeting places for starving singles, home-business operators and extended families, as well as for visitors. Minds have been opened to the fascinating fusions of food Australian kitchens have created.

Little eateries, often licensed, colourful, highly visible and producing affordable, fashionable fare, have caused a cultural culinary revolution that began in the mid '80s. Prior to that tastebud explosion, our rather predictable Celtic eating patterns were home-based, with a night out meaning the pub or club, often a family and neighbourly weekend barbecue in the backyard with choices of limited imagination dished out by Mum under firm instructions from Dad. Big celebratory milestones in life were marked in a restaurant or posh hotel dining room or even those bastions of respectability - department store canteens and grand railway refreshment rooms.

Still, it takes time to build a food culture and although Brisbane people have enthusiastically embraced the new eateries and the cafe scene, there is still not much culinary depth in Brisbane. This becomes evident when you note the lack of fresh local produce stores available. Visitors could expire from scurvy while trying to find a fresh fruit or vegie shop, and the one only fresh vegie market (Rocklea) is too hard to get to and not very inspiring if by chance you do find it. It seems that there is, as yet, no great interest in the elements, the ingredients of the food – it's more in the event of eating it.

$	(Inexpensive)	Under $15
$$	(Moderate)	$15-$35
$$$	(High)	$35-$50
$$$$	(Expensive)	$50+

(Per person - drinks extra)

Pricing and opening times

When it comes to prices, we believe all our recommendations to be good value for money, regardless of their cost. These days, most places take credit cards, so we no longer make a special note of this. Some places close on Monday, but most are open every day. Hours can vary, so it is best to check in advance, especially for lunch.

BRISBANE'S BEST TABLES

Here is a list of eateries that shows the great variety in style and nationality we now have. They range from the most expensive to the not-so-expensive (we have a separate section on cheap eats). What they all have in common, however, is that Brisbane foodies have nominated them as Brisbane's Best Tables.

Aix Bistro $

83 Merthyr Road, New Farm
Tel 3358 6444   Licensed

You can stop puckering up your mouth, they pronounced it "ex" as in "X", after owner Michel Thompson's favourite town in France, Aix en Provence. This pleasant, unpretentious bistro is new on the Brisbane scene but we believe it will be around for a long time. Thompson, who pioneered Brisbane's sidewalk cafe society with Le Scoops in the early '80s, has established an easy, open environment with the kind of simple quality food and service that attracts top chefs, such as Philip Johnson and Paul Hoffman, on their days off. Great value for money. Both outdoor and air-conditioned sections.

Baguette Restaurant $$$

French/Australian
150 Racecourse Road, Ascot
Tel 3268 6168   Licensed

Brasserie with an art gallery. Inside and outdoor seating. Multiple award-winning Brisbane classic near the airport in a smart street. Try the Thai red curry, or sambal prawns on lime-scented coconut rice and creamed pawpaw, or chicken breast with spiced coriander sauce and star anise, or poached pears with black tea-poached prunes. Diners are nurtured with professional service and personal attention from members of the Domenech family.

Bistrot One $$

561 Brunswick Street, New Farm
Tel 3358 3600   Optional BYO

Craig and Leisa Warren's dramatic, arty eatery is getting a rave from locals for its modern Australian cuisine. There's a small and highly creative menu with great attention to the wine list and recommendations, as well as champagnes, sparkling and still wines by the glass. Easy parking.

Cafe Citrus $$

Modern Australian
161 Oxford Street, Bulimba
Tel 3899 0242   BYO

Good honest food served simply and well, in a busy, interesting area near the River. A hit with locals who race in between movies (there are two cinemas close by), encouraging the kitchen to produce their favourites at very odd hours. "We cook when they want to eat and why not? That's what these suburban places should do," says the owner. Best-loved dishes are beef fillet stacked with wilted spinach, steak-and-kidney pie with mash and jus, and roast pumpkin risotto with rocket and crisp-fried polenta. Pray the banana waffles with honey and hazelnut ice cream are still on the menu.

Cha Cha Char $$$
Wine Bar and Grill
Eagle Street Pier, 1 Eagle Street, City
Tel 3211 9944   Licensed
Superb steaks with full descriptions on what breed and where they came from, along with damn fine onions and mustards, red wine and plenty of other excellent offerings delight Cha Cha's discriminating customers. A wood-fired oven that's fueled with old apple sticks does good bread.

Continental Cafe $$$
Modish Bistro
21 Barker Street, New Farm
Tel 3254 0377   BYO/licensed
A haunt of movers and shakers, rich and famous, who slum it here makeup-less and in their old clothes, for informal meetings and greetings. Open all day until late. Guests treat their well-mannered offspring to rich puds or crisp, thick chips. Small but excellent menu, crazy kitchen on show, where bustling attendants perform some interesting theatre. Opposite a serious cinema and fine bookshop, and next to flower and flour (bakery) shops. Try the oriental crab salad, designer pizzas, seafood pot-au-feu, or veal shanks, and close with pear and treacle pudding with caramel sauce.

Customs House Brasserie $$$
399 Queen Street, City
Tel 3365 8921   Licensed
Cake and coffee with culture or innovative international cuisine in Heritage

surroundings or on the Terrace overlooking the Story Bridge, your choice. Go by CityCat to the River Boardwalk and take a tour of the interiors afterwards with a guide on this inner-city treasure of a building.

e'cco $$$
Modern Australian
100 Boundary and Adelaide streets, City
Tel 3831 8344   Licensed
Awarded 1997 Australian Restaurant of the Year (*Gourmet Traveller*/Remy Martin Award. Leading priority for discerning gourmet travellers seeking beautifully crafted, wholesome meals done in front of them by a master - food to make them feel good rather than full, from a menu where everything cries out to be tasted. Philip Johnson is owner-chef. His attitude to simplicity and perfection, permeates this disciplined cafe near the Story Bridge in a building that was once a tea warehouse. Eat everything in sight on site.

Ed and Mary's $$
Cafe and Wine Bar
cnr Mary and Edward Street, City
Tel 3229 6606
Heritage building that serves local heritage fare in the manner of the old country homes but with a delicious modern twist. A Queensland feeling here with genuine comfort food served in welcoming casual surroundings that will give travellers a snapshot flash of the good old days of calm Country Life. Part of its attraction is that it is such a delightful meeting place.

Emporio $$
Eagle Street Pier, 1 Eagle Street, City
Tel 3229 9915   Licensed
Next door to Il Centro and also owned by the Andy and Marcia George, this small,

well-loved, voguish Italian bar serves coffee and food of the style usually found in Milan, Venice and Florence. Divine breakfasts and very smart informal lunches with Italian breads taken straight from the ovens. Coffee here is very special. Good meeting place to sit outside and watch the passing parade of people and river boats while sitting in the sun.

FW Canteen $
352 Brunswick Street, Fortitude Valley
Tel 3252 2956   BYO
Mediterranean
Kate Winter created a hit in Sydney with Winter-on-Crown and she's obviously doing the same with FW Canteen in Brisbane. This is where some of the city's top chefs go on their day off. The food? "Mediterranean/ vegetarian, modern type of food, very fresh." In fact, vegetables are so central to the menu that they are even represented in the decor. The restaurant is tiny, with steel-topped tables but on a hot night you can sit at tables outside on the pavement.

Grape Wine and Food Bar $$$
1st Floor, 308 Wickham Street, Fortitude Valley
Tel 3852 1618
The historic Wickham Hotel, a thriving gay pub, is very proud of its little bistro upstairs, which shares limited space with a wine bar, art gallery, mysteriously crowded corridors, rickety staircases and strangely slanted verandahs. The small menu is distinguished by simple and imaginative renderings of creative, homely fare, such as goat cheese ravioli with pear compote, tomato extract and black pepper, or bonded backstrap of lamb on green rice with charred eggplant and balsamic glaze. The bistro has received accolades of "Most Interesting New Restaurant" from local food and wine reviewers and the "Best Small Restaurant Wine List in Queensland". You can buy wine here by the quarter-glass to test your palate's progress.

Green Papaya $$
North Vietnamese
898 Stanley Street, East Brisbane
Tel 3217 3599   BYO (wine only)
High-quality ingredients feature in the authentic, aromatic, fresh food cooked by

Lien Yeomans (the chef/proprietor, pictured above with son, Quan). Food is served by her in bright and colourful indoor/outdoor surroundings. Very popular and buzzy spot with menu advice from enthusiastic staff for those unfamiliar with the nuances of North Vietnamese cuisine. Not surprisingly, the green papaya salad, pillow cakes and spicy prawns in coconut, chilli, lemongrass and garlic are rarely allowed to leave the menu. Open for dinner every night (except Monday); lunch "by appointment only".

Il Centro $$$
Modern Italian
Eagle Street Pier, 1 Eagle Street, City
Tel 3221 6090   Licensed
A consistently excellent, multiple award-winning, busy restaurant that would be more

at home in old Rome than new downtown Brisbane. Almost on the River with a great passing parade of boats, lights and people. A lovely place to linger and soak up the essence of the city and the river breezes with wine and antipasti. The seasonal menu offers excellent fare - favourites are the sand-crab ravioli, fresh Atlantic salmon chargrilled with mashed red pepper compote and citrus hollandaise, or chicken and tomato tossed with baby mozzarella on spaghetti and olive tapenade. For dessert, hand-crafted gelato or semi freddo with vanilla, butterscotch and honeycomb.

Il Centro

Isis Brasserie $$

446 Brunswick Street, Fortitude Valley
Tel 3852 1155   Licensed
Here is dedicated cooking without pretension. Walk into the light and simple ambience of this fairly new entry to Eat Street in the Valley and you'll probably find owners Simon Hill and Scott Perry at the helm. In the semi-open kitchen Jason Cohen creates the attractive combinations and eclectic flavours of Asia and southern Europe we now recognise as Modern Australian cuisine. The selection of wines, by glass or bottle, is impressive, except we missed a local entry. Prices are reasonable and, in a bid to keep

them that way, life's little luxuries, such as bugs and crabs, are often left off the menu. So when you ring to book (and we suggest you do that a couple of days ahead) check whether the bugs are on. Parking is reasonable in Brunswick Street.

> ### THE HEAT IN THE KITCHEN
> *Battle lines are being drawn up in Brissie between customers and restaurateurs.*
> #### NO 1
> Gone is the humble veg. Customers wonder whatever happened to serving good fresh green vegetables with their meal. It seems that the better the establishment and the bigger the bill, the less visible is the humble veg. Most-seen green in recent times has been wilted bok choy.

The Malaysian Experience $$

80 Jephson Street, Toowong
Tel 3870 2646   Licensed
Tucked away down an alley beside a huge supermarket carpark in the Legal and General Building, this place is popular for its consistently good Malaysian fare. Enjoys the accolade of "best representative of authentic Malaysian cuisine". Try the noodles, seafood specialties, laskas, curries and claypot chicken. Trust the specialties of the award-winning chef, who once cooked for Malaysian royalty.

Marco Polo Restaurant $$$$

Level 2, Treasury Casino, Queen Street, City
Tel 3306 8744   Licensed
Quality dining spot with the disadvantage that you have to walk through the Casino to get there. Try the Peking duck or the oriental

stir-fries, seafood and noodles with classically spiced sauces. Choose between chargrilled beef, Japanese sashimi or Malaysian laksa hotpot. The Singapore chilli mud crab with deep-fried buns and Asian salad is excellent, too. Decor is grand but not overwhelming, and the service sensitive and unobtrusive in this historic chunk of the state's original Treasury Building. One of five Queensland restaurants mentioned in the Australian "Wine List of the Year" award. Downstairs is a fun cafe called Luigi Pastrano, Asian Italian and worth a look at the decor and loud carpets.

Medium Rare $$
French/Australian
102 Kedron Road, North Wilston
Tel 3856 5588
In the suburb of North Wilston, is a good place for steaks, seafood and a superb bouillabaisse. It's run by Thierry Galichet, late of Indigo, and is open every night.

Michael's Riverside Restaurant $$$$
Mediterranean
Riverside Centre, 123 Eagle Street, Brisbane
Tel 3881 5522   Licensed
Michael Platsis' beloved fine dining room on the best riverfront site in town boasts superb views. Pleasant up-to-date food, interesting people and airy, expensive decor provide an energetic buzz. European opulence with full silver-service extravagance. Michael also has a good cellar.

Pier Nine Oyster Bar and Seafood Grill $$$$

Eagle Street Pier, 1 Eagle Street, City
Tel 3229 2194   Licensed
Seafood served up on the curve of the River where the original Port of Brisbane once stood. This appealing local experience offers

cool breezes and sweeping views in an informal setting that suits visitors' need to see a real regional specialty. Many awards for excellences, such as oysters from Nambucca Heads, Moreton Bay and elsewhere, shucked to order. Fish is extremely fresh and the mud crabs are cooked to perfection. Large bowls of Thai noodles and caesar salad are now a trademark - a macho-size rump steak and an aged rib-roast on the bone are popular, but it's the seafood that stars here. Comprehensive wine list with some local wines.

Pine and Bamboo $$$
Chinese
968 Wynnum Road, Cannon Hill
Tel 3399 9095   Licensed
Although this large restaurant hides in a small suburb, it offers a fine Peking duck. As well, the mermaid's tresses, roast pork and live seafood of all kinds give an indication of its extensive menu. Devoted pilgrims from even the outer reaches of Brisbane make the trip to enjoy quality Chinese food here. The deep-fried shredded beef tastes much grander than it sounds, and an intelligent but modestly priced wine list is well suited to the fare.

Romeo's $$$$
Italian
216 Petrie Terrace, City
Tel 3367 0955   Licensed Bar
Many Brisbane foodies have nominated Romeo's as the best in town for voguish home-cooking styles of generously filling food. Owner-chef Romeo Riga encourages enthusiastic eating in true Italian style, with punters sharing from platters and relying on his personal advice regarding the day's best offerings from the markets. Quintessentially Italian food with Australian ingredients, selections include pasta with bugs, tomatoes,

shallots, and fresh asparagus, with side dishes of chilli and parmesan (tagliarini al' Aragosta), or mussels steamed in their own juice with garlic, shallots, white wine and chilli (cozzealla Veneziana). There's an extensive range of Italian and Australian wines.

Senso Unico $$$
92-96 Merthyr Road, New Farm
Tel 3358 6644   Licensed
Well-known in Noosa where they ran a restaurant in Hastings Street, Peter Reddie and Garry George have brought a fresh, clean-cut Italianate look to their newest establishment. The fish stew is excellent.

Shingle Inn $$
254 Edward Street, City
Tel 3221 9039   BYO
This never-changing inner-city icon is a blast from the past for generations of locals. They hold this quaint tea room dear and sneak back to rekindle childhood memories. The American Forces during the WWII introduced Shingle Inn cooks to crisp waffles (the irons are still imported from the USA), salads and hot or iced milky coffee. Only the prices and uniforms have changed in 50 years. Cakes are superb, buy some at the front desk to take home. The waffles with butterscotch sauce are very special and so, too, are the fresh sand-crab or chicken sandwiches, roast of the day or pork sausages and mash.

Siggi's At The Port Office $$$$
Grand Dining and Wine Bar
Heritage Hotel, Edward Street, City
Tel 3221 4555   Licensed
The magnificent old colonial bar at the top of the mahogany staircase is a must. Meet people there and order a champagne and

oysters supper. Siggi's beautiful dining room for more swept-up customers is adjacent. Once the original Brisbane Port Office near the Botanic Gardens, now a boutique hotel

The back-room boys at Siggis.

on the River, it also sports a very cool brasserie, famous for its breakfasts and brunches. Siggi's favourites might be the "windows concept" (a bit of everything), or asparagus and crab salad with caviar creme fraiche, or simple loin of spring lamb on roasted marinated eggplant with a pinot pan jus. Desserts are seductive, particularly anything chocolate - and you can have the entire meal sent to your hotel room to eat in bed! Great wine list.

Tables of Toowong $$$
Modern Australian
88 Miskin Street, Toowong
Tel 3371 4558   Licensed
With possibly the sharpest reputation of any chef in Brisbane, ex-Melbournite Russell Armstrong is the high-octane tower of power and creativity that drives this much-acclaimed and awarded temple to good food and cheffing. Hidden away in a dippy street in suburban Toowong, 10 minutes' drive from the city heart, this is the place to take an educated palate. An imaginative and well-matched wine list produces a polished buzz. All dishes also come in entree sizes.

Two Small Rooms $$$
French/Mediterranean
517 Milton Road, Toowong
Tel 3371 5251   BYO
Everybody in the industry eats here, including many of the city's chefs, which is always a good sign. Owner Michael Conrad and leading chef David Pugh offer French-style cuisine with Asian and Mediterranean influences in this admirably restored old corner shop, 10 minutes from the city. The menu changes regularly but some things, such as the specialty souffles, are always included. Chicken and Moreton Bay bugs with Moroccan spices on couscous are recommended by management, as is the utterly desirable caramelised mango and white chocolate marque.

BEN'S CHEAP EATS
If less than $15 for a main course means inexpensive by our criteria, then Ben's Cheap Eats is in the give-away category.

Aloha

Chinatown Mall,
Fortitude Valley
Excellent, cheap Chinese/Malaysian. Light on for atmosphere and they just about throw the food at you, but hard to beat as value for the money.

Chez Laila
Boardwalk, South Bank (at the Maritime Museum end)
Tel 3846 3402
A welcome presence in an area short on good places to eat. If you're looking for a hearty breakfast with a difference, try one here. It's hearty (flatbread, feta, tiny black olives, great coffee) and good value.

Kadoya
Shop 30, Elizabeth St Arcade (99 Elizabeth Street, City)
Tel 3229 3993
Authentic Japanese Sushi Bar, but you'll have to fight the Japanese for a place to sit down.

Khan's Kitchen
75 Hardgrave Road, West End
Tel 3844 0877
An alfresco Pakistani restaurant - very cheap and fast, authentic and friendly. Kenneth Pervez, owner and chef is often seen out on the street chatting with patrons.

THE HEAT IN THE KITCHEN
Battle lines are being drawn up in Brissie between customers and restaurateurs.
NO 2
Open wide. There are complaints that food voguishly stacked like high-rise towers on the plate doesn't fit into average-size mouths without their owners jaws becoming front-loading washing machines on the full-wash cycle. This is not at all becoming to watch.

King Ahiram's
88 Vulture Street, West End
Tel 3846 1678
Lebanese, very quick and easy takeaway. Authentic and fresh. You may have to wait in line a bit in busy periods.

New Wing Hing BBQ
187 Wickham Street, City
Tel 3252 4100
The chap who cooks here says that you cannot spell char siu lom mein (BBQ pork

and noodles) in English because it is spelled differently in four or five parts of China and there is only one England.

Palace Cafe
Ann Street, City
Tel 3211 9277
Attached to the Palace Backpackers Hostel, this is a good, all-purpose cafe, coveniently located.

Satay Club Cafe
66 Charlotte Street, City
Tel 3229 8855
This is an early opener (not Sunday) for authentic Malaysian. Very quick service, cheap and damn good. Char kway chow is recommended.

Tibetan Kitchen
454 Brunswick Street, Fortitude Valley
Tel 3358 5906
Quite cheap. We suggest you try the poleko kukhuwra - whole or half chook, boned and marinated in yoghurt and lemon and cooked in a tandoori oven. Vegie stuff, too.

Pub food

Brisbane pubs and clubs were once, and still are, terrific value because the grog trade always subsidised the food. Steaks that overlapped large plates were common, always served with mountains of chips, grated beetroot, onion rings, cubes of cheese and a watery iceberg salad on the side.

While meat and two veg is still a fixed Queensland expectation for most people, it's now quite likely to be a stir-fry with everything combined in a wok. Today's menu could easily be a Thai chicken curry, Lebanese dips with hot Turkish bread, steamed local seafood wrapped in bark or chargrilled. Or maybe Middle-eastern kebabs on aubergine, instead of the rissoles, or a roast-of-the-day with brown gravy and watery veg that once fed the nation.

Staff are mostly attractive, smart, young and restless, well on their studious ways to better careers. They've replaced the old-time, gloriously mature creatures who would beam and say with genuine feeling, "Git that inta ya then, dear" or "This should set youse up for the die, love". All meals once came laden with pineapple rings, orange twists or a forest of parsley and piles of buttered bread but now, even in bistros, you order potatoes, vegetables and bread as extras with a price tag.

Beer in Brisbane

Bulimba Gold Top, as displayed on our cover by Mrs J. H. Rogers, the charming daughter of the chairman of Queensland Brewery, was the famous old-time Brisbane beer. However, like so many local endeavours, it was taken over by the big boys and no longer exists. The defiantly branded XXXX is the traditional beer now, although that excellent drop also seems to be under threat from a southerner's brand, Victorian Bitter. The old folk don't approve.

Wine in Brisbane

It's not that Brisbane people don't drink wine, far from it. In any of the restaurants and cafes we have recommended in this book you will find good wine lists, wine by the glass or an appreciative acceptance of BYO. It's just that all the wines on the list will be from Tasmania, Victoria, New South Wales, South and Western Australia or even New Zealand - you'll be lucky to find any wines from Queensland.

Our untourist credo is all about looking for the best of the local product, so this makes a piece on local wines in Brisbane a bit hard. Let it be known that here are wines grown and made in Queensland - it's just that they're not recognised as being as good as the wines from other parts of Australia - not yet, anyway. The main reason is the climate. Great wines tend not to come from hot regions. Now, having said that, the best of them are grown not far from Brisbane in the Granite Belt near Stanthorpe. Sicilians settled here in the early 1900s and the area now scoops the pool in wine awards and cannot keep up with the demand - often selling out at the cellar back door to visitors before they have time to fill orders for restaurants in other states. In Brisbane, you'll find these wines at Grape Liquor Markets.

Rimfire Winery of Maclaga in northeastern Darling Downs, and Ballandean Estate have won several local awards (they make an excellent dessert wine "Silvania"). Other developing wineries - Riverlands at St George, Golden Grove and Heritage at Stanthorpe, and Romaville in Roma. Most are growing Italian grapes for Lambrusca wines, using sangiovese, nebbiolo, barbera, pinot grigio and tarangro grape varieties. The Robinson family estate makes a good methode champenoise, Preston Peak a shiraz, Stone Ridge a malbec and Bungawarra a chardonnay in a seasonal vintage of about 860 tonnes. Tip from Philip Johnson is the semillon from Barambah's Ridge.

Closer to home is the new vinery at Mt Tamborine, which is now exporting to Asia. The Burnett district is also the promised land for grapes and we will soon be swamped with good regional wines. All these vineyards welcome visitors for discussion tours and tastings.

Brisbane has a wine festival in early November at the Brisbane Convention and Exhibition Centre in South Brisbane, covering everything you can never really absorb in one visit. It is enlightening to see what is available and coming on stream, however. The famous Ekka, or Royal Agricultural Exhibition, is held in early August and has a wine show that almost takes the cake. While the judging is being done, locals can buy a ticket to join in the serious tastings and watch the judges spitting out liquid loveliness.

THE BRUCE HOOD PUB TRAIL

Bruce Hood (above), aka Bluey Tucker, publican, truckie and poet, blew out of the west half a century ago. Ever since he's been old enough to be allowed in, he's been racking up all the credentials necessary to write about Queensland pubs. He's eaten in them, drunk in them, sung in them, brawled in them, been thrown out of them and even run a couple. More bard than boozer, Bruce now lives a quiet life in the Brisbane suburbs with his wife, his vintage tractors and his word processor.

Here is Bruce Hood's selection of the best pubs in Brisbane :

Australian National
Cnr Wellington Street, Woolloongabba
Tel 3391 3964
A gutsy hotel close to the city where customers such as Snow, who has been a client for 40 years, rub shoulders with the lively Aussie Rules crowd from the adjacent Gabba stadium. In the large TAB you can see Queensland's greatest scholars of form at work, researching their infallible betting systems. The Guinness bar is a beauty. It's like an old gentleman's club in atmosphere, with a well-polished timber decor and soft, easy lighting. But don't let that fool you, because on Friday and Saturday nights it is alive and well with great middle-of-the-road entertainment. There are 20 old-style pub rooms with ample off-street parking. A cab to the city is $5 or there are buses at the door. Terry Morrow, the boss, and friendly staff will make you feel at home at the "Aussie Nosh" if a good near-city pub is your bag.

Grand View Hotel
49 North Street, Cleveland Point
Tel 3286 1002
This aptly named hotel offers wide views of Moreton Bay and its islands. Continually licensed since 1887, it is the state's longest serving hotel. Sea breezes cool guests in summer and open fires warm their bones in winter. Great meals and beverages are served in a range of bars and rooms from outdoors to private dining areas. Music covers a range from jazz in the garden to a grand piano in the dining room. There's always something

happening, from a regular magician to bridge classes. Plenty on- and off-street parking. The Grand View is an ideal centre from which to explore the Redland area and the bay islands.

Hamilton Hotel

Grand View Hotel, Cleveland Point.

South Drive, Hamilton
Tel 32268 7500
The Hamilton is a big-capacity modern one-stop entertainment facility. There are six bars, including a nightclub, and live entertainment is offered in all of them. There are bands on Thursday, Friday, Saturday and Sunday nights, sometimes in multiples until late. Food is bistro-style and good. The pub's own bus leaves for the city at 3.15am Friday and Saturday nights. It can be booked to pick up and deliver home your party of 20 or more.

Jubilee Hotel
470 St Paul's Terrace, Fortitude Valley
Tel 3252 4508
If you were gently raised and are unfortunate enough not to have grown out of it, keep away from the Jubilee, especially during Ekka (10-20 August), after the game at Ballimore, or in the breeding season. On the other hand, if you like to take your meat from the maws of lions, this rip-roaring country pub in the city is your Mecca. Owned by former Wallaby Chris (The Buddha) Handy, who

on unrehearsed occasions has been known to be the star turn, this is a fun pub. There is always something on the boil when the mob is in town. Also dangerous are Friday and Saturday nights. The bistro serves real tucker in man-size portions. A crown jewel among worthy waterholes and about six bucks in a cab from the city centre.

Manly Hotel
Cnr Cambridge Pde and Station Terrace, Manly
Tel 3396 8188
The Manly, a classic early post-war hotel, has been run by the McDonald family for three generations. Situated in the heart of Manly village, the yacht harbour, several sailing and boating clubs, jetties, marinas and launching ramps are all close by. Lively, well patronised by locals, visiting tradesmen, untourists and boaties using the bay, it is a popular destination. On-street and off-street parking. Top-class bars offer all modern facilities, including gaming, TAB, cable and satellite sport. There is a range of food from bar meals to fine dining and function facilities. A wide range of entertainment is offered six nights a week plus Saturday and Sunday afternoons. A circular bus route connects with the electric train to Brisbane - 25 minutes. The Manly is a well-run, high-standard traditional Aussie pub.

Royal Exchange
10 High Street, Toowong
Tel 3371 2555
The Royal Exchange is an unpretentious fun pub where a cosmopolitan crowd covering three generations mixes easily in a friendly atmosphere. Seniors, university students and young business people from the adjacent Toowong shopping area relax or party in air-conditioned comfort. The beer garden is a popular luncheon venue. Reasonable prices, interesting menus that change daily, and generous portions are part of the customer-friendly attitude. On Fridays, the business luncheon starts a gathering that ends as a lively, packed celebration of the end of the working week and at 6pm a wooden keg of cold beer is broached. Unplugged, easy-listening music six nights as week. The Royal Exchange offers all modern facilities. Toowong station is a few steps away and it is just two stations from Roma Street. A great place to relax.

Queens Arms Hotel
64 James Street, Teneriffe
Tel 3358 2799
The Queen's Arms has one of the last, intact, true local bars close to the CBD. It is the locals' local. The public bar is their domain. I lived close by for several years and often made a Saturday-morning foray before lunch. It is vintage old Brisbane. There are also two up-market bars in which Rugby is spoken and understood. The food is great and prices are real value. Hostess Donna's spaghetti with oysters and chilli has won a *Courier Mail* Pub Recipe Award. It is a popular business luncheon port of call. A cab from the city costs five or six bucks. In the evening, journos can be found muttering in a corner or doing tricks at the bar. It is a pub where interesting developments, often with no prompting, take on a life of their own. Well worth a visit.

ICON EATERIES
In every city in the world there are certain places that have become an intrinsic part of the local eating or drinking scene. They may not fit into Brisbane's Best Tables selection or have the best view, but they cannot be ignored. In Brisbane, the following list of

establishments fit these criteria.

City Gardens Cafe $

City Botanic Gardens

Alice and George streets (Best entrance via Gardens Point Road)

Tel 3229 1554   Licensed

This charming and unpretentious little place, the original caretaker's cottage of the Botanic Gardens, was built in 1855. You can now eat on the terrace overlooking the gardens and the tropical rainforest. The food is fresh, unpretentious and never boring. Hearty breakfasts, light lunches (featuring what they term gourmet sandwiches), traditional Devonshire teas, espresso coffees and cakes are available all day. For dinner, book first to make sure nobody is having a wedding reception. Air-conditioned.

Breakfast Creek Hotel $

2 Kingsford Smith Drive, Breakfast Creek

Tel 3262 5988

If you're in the mood for steak and beer, go

no farther. A good pub atmosphere and old ghosts of the Left - this is where the Australian Labor Party held its national convention for many years. To get there, just head for the

airport on Route 25 and park your Hog out the back.

California Cafe $$

376 Brunswick Street, Fortitude Valley

Tel 3852 1026   BYO

Lainey Lonergan and son Jack have cleverly preserved the original 1950s milk-bar decor in this elderly historic landmark cafe that has seen better days but is still great fun for breakfast on weekends. Huge plates of breakfast-style food of the type beloved by real working men of that bygone era (baked beans, spaghetti on toast, etc.), but all homemade. Try the Truckie's Platter, eggs Benedict or even bubble-and-squeak.

Gambaro's

33 and 34 Caxton Street, Petrie Terrace

Tel 3369 9500

Michael Gambaro's father arrived from Italy in 1937. When war was declared, he was promptly interned as a prisoner of war. In the mid '50s, the family bought a couple of shops in Caxton Street, one of which was a fish-and-chip shop. They now have Brisbane seafood sewn up ("by the short and curlies," says Michael). They own the fish market at 1173 Kingsford Smith Drive, Eagle Farm, and a major fish-importing business. The Caxton Street shops are now a seafood takeaway and oyster bar on one side of the road and the edifice-like, dress-up, sit-down licensed fish restaurant across the road.

Jameson's

Restaurant and Bar

475 Adelaide Street, City

Tel 3831 7633

Jameson's is too young to be a Brisbane icon really, as James Brotherstone started this great place only 15 months ago - but it is clearly a Brisbane tradition in the making and we thoroughly recommend it. Many modern eateries are so cool they're cold, Jameson's is not your chic designer place, it is stimulating, warm and the people there care about the food, the wine, the jazz, literary readings, debates or whatever is going on at the time. It's holed up in a nice old building in an interesting little precinct of Brisbane with a great view of the River. The fresh, simple food is cooked with panache. Ask about **Wordpool**, an occasional and innovative "literary cabaret" at Jameson's— fast paced, instructive, confronting and funny. (See 8 THE ARTS).

THE HEAT IN THE KITCHEN

Battle lines are being drawn up in Brissie between customers and restaurateurs.

NO 3

"Cakeage" has now been added to "corkage". Restaurant owners might countercharge the public with sharp arguments against constant no shows, rudeness, no tipping, hostility toward corkage and now cakeage. Many are dead against allowing BYO birthday cakes with the expectation of plates and cutlery being provided free. Inroads into profits from rejected dessert menus have now made cakeage complaints overtake the debate on smoking and breast-feeding in public. Mark our words, there will be icing flowing in the streets very soon.

Le Scoops

Ice cream parlour and cafe
283 Given Terrace, Paddington
Tel 3368 2640
(The ice cream is also franchised out to Le Scoops at 200 Old Cleveland Road, Coorparoo, and 9 Sherwood Road, Toowong)

A pioneer of the Brisbane sidewalk cafe society that arrived in the mid '80s and has exploded over the city in the past 10 years. ("Soon there will be a cafe for each of us," quips Brisbane's very savvy local foodie Jan Power.) Locals claim Le Scoops is the best ice cream in town and probably the best in the state. Owner Michel Thompson doesn't use imported "starters" for his wonderful ice cream and sorbets, everything starts from ingredients on the premises. The chocolate is the best ever, and the mango sorbet takes a lot of beating. They sometimes make tropical exotica, such as moonflower cactus or black sapote ice cream, when these Queensland fruits are in season.

Red Cross Tea Rooms $

Basement, Brisbane City Hall, Adelaide Street, City
Tel 3403 8888 (City Council enquiries)
Frozen in time and staffed by volunteers, this

is probably the last vestige of Brisbane's war years. The tea rooms attract regular customers and staff with very plain edibles totally devoid of any fascinating diversity. The tea is from a giant urn and the sandwiches and scones are made by the nice ladies of the Red Cross. Around the walls are photos of wartime Brisbane and also some strange, but sort of appealing things you can buy. Tea $1, Scones about $2, but don't ask for a cappuccino or a latte. Don't miss this proper, historic, Brisbane icon.

FOOD TRIPS

There are some worthwhile foodie treats to buy in and out of the city. Brisbane is close to "the bread basket of Queensland" - the Darling Downs - and also to the area around Noosa where exotic produce is grown. We have listed a few of the best places here for gastronomic explorers, but we deal with food trips in more detail in another of our publications, *Untourist Queensland*.

A trip west of Brisbane to the Darling Downs will allow you to dip into a cornucopia of goodies. Near Gatton, on the way to Toowoomba, there are some great fruit and vegie stands that sell local produce grown in the area - avocados, mangos and those wonderfully sweet little pineapples when they're in season. In Toowoomba, try the Roslyn Horrobin's Caboolture blue cheese - it's like a good Castello. The wonderful Weis frozen food factory is in Toowoomba, and has now been there for 40 years, making their fruit ice blocks and tubs of yummy mango Frutia (a bit like gelato). You can buy their products at local supermarkets, milkbars, etc. You could also stay on the Weis family trail and eat lunch at their "eat-till-you-drop" icon, **Weis Restaurant** - ask anyone in Toowoomba where it is. Anything from the Toowoomba company **Mother Meg** is to be grabbed immediately. They produce biscuits and great puddings for gourmets and sweet toothers. Products are also available in most supermarkets throughout Brisbane.

Heading south from Brisbane on the way to the Gold Coast, you will pass, on the right-hand side, the most famous pie place in the state, **Yatala Pies**. Watch out for the big pie in the sky to indicate the shop, and join the line of truckies, families and Japanese surfies for a fine Aussie pie. But before you get too excited, check our website updates because Yatala Pies could be under threat from a planned multi-lane highway, Macphersons Road, Yatala.

Just 30 minutes east from the centre of Brisbane, heading for the sea, you'll find yourself at **Morgan's Seafood**, Scarborough. Since the '70s, there's always been a Morgan on the boat harbour. It started with a simple

Morgan's Seafood, Scarborough.

fisherman selling his catch, to a fish market, to an excellent takeaway and restaurant with full seafood menu and an Asian Grill. But make sure you book ahead. Morgans is probably still the best fish shop in Brisbane. Join the Brisbane devotees and line up for fish straight from the trawlers.
Bird O' Passage Parade. Scarborough,

Old lighthouse is better than the new.

The Mirosches and their two silly dogs.

At the very tip of Cleveland Point, the **Lighthouse Restaurant Bar and Cafe** is set in an 1850s Customs House, between the old and the new lighthouses. The Bar can get very buzzy on Friday and Saturday nights, but it's usually a good crowd. You don't have to book, but if you want a table with a good view of Moreton, Peel and North Stradbroke Islands, book well in advance. 237 Shore Street.

If you decide to go for a wonderful inexpensive dinner (the only meal available) at **Blue Water** on North Stradbroke Island, good luck, because it is somewhat complicated to get there and even more complicated to get back - in fact you can't. The last ferry leaves before dinner so you'd best plan to stay overnight. (see 13 OUT OF BRISBANE). Andrew Mirosch has a hands-on approach, greeting customers, seating them and taking the orders. Andrew set up here because he loves the lifestyle and likes to live where he works. An excellent, all-round, seafood-based menu, and well worth the effort, Endeavour Street, Point Lookout, North Stradbroke Island.

Pioneers

Philip Johnson one of the brave pioneer chefs of Brisbane. The ones who have put themselves (and their money in many cases) on the line and pushed up the standards. Some of them like **Gillian Hurst** and **Anne** and **Doug Flockhart** have left the scene, but there are still some of the innovators who are now reaping the rewards – as well they should: **Russell Armstrong**, Tables of Toowong; **David Pugh** of Two Small Rooms and **Michel Thompson** who was probably the first mover and shaker in the sidewalk cafe scene around 1983, although Michel gives credit to **Aroma** who started at about the same time.

Pioneers, cont'd

BUG AND FENNEL RISSOTTO WITH LEMON OIL *Philip Johnson*
Ingredients
18 Moreton Bay bugtails, shelled
1.25 litres chicken stock
50ml olive oil
1 fennel bulb, sliced
2 teaspoons fennel seeds, roasted an crushed
half teaspoon dried chilli
4 golden shallots, peeled and diced (or 1 onion)
2 cloves garlic, crushed
1 and a half cups Arborio rice
100gm parmesan, freshly grated
30gm butter
half lemon, juice only
quarter cup flatleaf parsley, washed and finely chopped
shaved parmesan
lemon oil
salt and pepper

Philip Johnson (top)
Michel Thompson (below)

Prepare bugtails by slicing into 2cm medallions. Bring chicken stock to the boil. Sweat fennel/fennel seeds, chilli, shallots and garlic in oil until shallots are transparent, lightly season. Add rice, stirring through until rice is well coated with oil. Increase heat, adding chicken sock a cup at a time, bring mixture to boil. Reduce heat to very low, continue adding stock by the cupful as required, stirring frequently. Continue this method until rice is almost cooked (approximately 30 minutes). Add the bugs to the risotto and simmer ;until bugs are just cooked through, fold in parmesan, butter, lemon juice to taste and parsley. Check seasonings and make sure mixture is not too wet (increase heat and allow liquid to evaporate if it is). Serve in bowls, topped with shaved parmesan and garnishing with pepper and a drizzle of lemon oil.

GUAVA SORBET
Michel Thompson
Ingredients
800gm of guavas will yield approximately 500gm of purée
500gm guava flesh — puréed and strained (necessary as flesh has grainy consistency)
Juice of one Lisbon lemon
1 desp. caster sugar
500ml sugar syrup (made from equal quantities of sugar and filtered water with the zest of one lemon)
1 egg white beaten soft (Optional)

Add guava purée, lemon juice and sugar and mix until sugar dissolved. Slowly add sugar syrup slowly to the mixture, testing the sweetness level of the product until it reaches 25°/26° Brix. This measurement can be made with a refractometer. Do NOT add all the sugar syrup. Once the sweetness level is reached put aside the syrup remaining. The egg white may be mixed through at this point. Put mixture into an icecream churn having turned on the refrigeration some 20 minutes beforehand. Churn until a smooth and thick consistency. Serve fresh.

11 Best
Things
to Buy

INCLUDES: *Where to get the best local product, including Murri artefacts; the Goanna Salve story; how to find the bargains; markets; shopping and the antiques circuit.*

This chapter has two aims – first, to guide you to the best shopping precincts (where to go to buy what) and second, to seek out the best products and services unique to Brisbane. We have fulfilled the first aim and done the best we could on the second as interesting locally designed or made products and ideas are, as yet, thin on the ground.

A FINE TRADITION

"In my youth, The Valley was the shopping centre in Brisbane. It was <u>the</u> place where children would go in the couple of weeks before Christmas to be entertained by the games and displays on top of McWhirters. It was where the commercial rivalry of McWhirters, T C Beirnes and Overells was considered a feature of Brisbane life", Jim Soorley, Lord Mayor of Brisbane, from the book *Two to the Valley* .

Most major cities have a retail tradition. In Australia, Melbourne has Myer, Sydney has David Jones and Gowings, Brisbane had the great rivalry between McWhirters and T C Beirnes which from the late 19th century, moved the major focus of retail trading in Brisbane from the CBD to Fortitude Valley, once described as the greatest commercial centre in Queensland.

In 1949 The Valley had a turnover of 15 million pounds, one third of which went through the tills of the big three department stores. This pattern remained until around 1960, when business wound down to a standstill due, apparently, to the younger family customers abandoning the near-city suburbs and moving out to pursue the Australian post-war dream of the quarter-acre block in the outer suburbs.

Brisbane has never regained its feet in retail since then and today the shops and department stores are dominated by the southern imports – Myer and David Jones, both of which are centred in the Queen Street Mall (below).

Small specialty shops selling good local products are also hard to find as Brisbane's new designers and creative entrepreneurs seem not to be making their presence felt at retail level as yet.

It's good news that major Australian and imported retail brands are available in Brisbane and a bit cheaper than in Melbourne or Sydney. The best small retailers seem to be bookshops (old, rare and new), Aboriginal (Murri) works shops (pictures, craft and weapons) and op shops.

ANTIQUES CIRCUIT

Rosebank Cottage is as good a place to start as any. A portrait of William White, the founder, as a young boy, hangs on the wall. Well-crafted waxed and stencilled country furniture each with an old penny (say, 1944, 1962) somewhere on the piece. All made from recycled Queensland timbers (some with ceiling mould panels). Each piece has a certificate of authentication with the origins of the wood, eg "this unique collection of timber was salvaged from Green Slopes Hospital Qld". A plaque has painted on it one of the founder's favourite quotes: *I love surprises, cold marble, candle light and the new moon. I like grapevines and ivy, simplicity, privacy.. My shade is pastel. I like white linen, listening to leaves and women who blush. I love to live for this moment, I love old dogs, inspiring words and jacarandas in November. I like the colour green, moss and rock pools* . 210 Mulgrave Road, Red Hill.

Paddington Antique Centre Open daily 10am–5pm. In an old theatre really chock full of stuff of all standards, 55 registered dealers, all under the one roof 167 Latrobe Terrace; **The Bardon Bazaar** is good for a browse through stuff with style, 78 MacGregor Terrace. There is a number of restoration stores in the circuit, the best one being **Poulos Restoration Station**, 98 Waterworks Road, Ashgrove. **Agent 029's** "TV cabinets and coffee tables (and the things they wear)" has mostly local art on the walls and some local furniture, but the overall flavour is imported. They have a catalogue of more than 200 things so order it if you can't find what you think you are looking for. The new furniture is hand-made from plantation mahogany. 29 Latrobe Terrace, Paddington.

The Old Paddington Store, Isabel, Keith (pictured) and Rowan Hatfield. Jam-packed with old stuff from old advertising and toys, a ship's telegraph to a newspaper front page declaring "Edward VIII Abdicates". These folk have been here since the dawn of time, and the collection reflects that. 19 Latrobe Terrace, 9.30am–4.30pm Wed, Thurs, Fri and Sat or by appointment.

Foresters Hall This is it, if you have money. A beautiful collection of unusual antiques, including 1.6 metre tall Armenian pots from Mount Ararat; large hand-carved Grecian columns 6.1 metres high, $2000 a set; Indian hand-carved church altar, an ecumenical steal at $12,000. Everything comes from Turkey, India and Greece, except the beds and sofas. 16 Latrobe Terrace, Paddington.

LOCAL PRODUCT

Fire-Works Gallery

(Aboriginal Art and other Burning issues). This discerning gallery is a commercial concern, though it offers support to artists in more ways than just showing art work. The mere existence of a credible and creative organisation that works as a commercial gallery without succumbing to the boomerang school of souvenirs, must give so much hope to indigenous artists. The National Gallery would be proud of the standard work on display. The gallery was set up by the Campfire Group in 1995, which began as an artist collective to support the art and to have a base in the city. They have established a network of Bush Studios in and around south-east Queensland for art production, workshops and cultural exchange. We have seen a few indigenous outlets and, be

Didgeridoos

assured, this one puts the art first (before the tourist dollars).

It has monthly feature exhibitions that pit new and up-coming artists with their more exposed peers. There is always something to buy, from original postcards to major works of sculpture or painting. There's a consultancy service for the more serious collector seeking particular works, or work from remote areas, 678 Ann Street, Fortitude Valley (near Brunswick Street Mall).

The **Contemporary Furniture Studio**, a 1860s a sheet-metal and tin smithy's workshop. The showroom displays a range of furniture, lighting, and useful or unusual items by local designers. A hand-made anodised aluminium ceiling fan from a Sunshine Coast designer has received international acclaim. In the workshop out back, two young designers are at work: Queensland's climate is reflected in furniture built with lightweight and renewable building materials by **Bruce Carrick**, while **Roy Shack** turns out antiques of the future. His motto for making fine furniture using traditional joinery techniques is: "Make it with love or don't make it at all", 16 Logan Road, Woolloongabba.

Didgeridoona.

This is an indigenous product like a portable Esky bag made of Drizabone-style canvas with leather handles and filled with Australian wool. It's a wine cooler, it works like a sheep, and it looks great. A must for the plonk porter. The makers of this product were very suspicious of our research (when we say we don't take any advertising, we really mean it). We haven't found it anywhere else but you can buy one at **Pamela's Pantry**, *Savoir Fair* Shop 6, Park Road, Milton. She also sells exquisite pantry food, pies, jams, pickles and a lot more (behind the Eiffel tower on Park Road.)

From Contemporary Art and Design Gallery.

Get your redback spider or blowfly bowtie from the **Contemporary Art and Design Gallery**. The gallery promotes the works of local artists and craftspeople. Pineapple earings and brooches of endangered, indigenous frogs are a colourful Queensland treat, 33 Logan Road, Woolloongabba.

THE MARKETS – A SUMMARY

There are a lot of markets to choose from, though they are not all good. Here are our choices: **Riverside** (Eagle Street Pier) Sunday 8am–3pm, **Brunswick Street Markets**, Fortitude Valley, Saturday 8am–2pm in the Brunswick Street Mall. They're a pretty big deal in The Valley on Saturday mornings. There's a stage in midway for good bands – nothing too one way or her other, but sophisticated stuff tailored to the mood and the buskers are pretty good too. Coffee shops everywhere including **Societe** where you can get a big bowl of latte (Betty Blue style); **South Bank Lantern and Craft** (really the same but the lantern is on Friday night); **Manly** Craft, The Esplanade, Manly Harbour Village, all day Sunday; **McWhirters**, Brunswick Street, Fortitude Valley, open every day 9am–4pm but the weekend is the time to go; **Ipswich Country** at the City Mall, all day on the first Sunday of each month.

South Bank Craft Markets

These markets are a bit touristy with a mix of run-of-the-mill market crafts and imports, with psychics, masseurs and palm readers scattered throughout. Up one end there's a chap who sells beautiful furniture. John Deshon's work (**Larrikin Furniture** – see page 166) includes prize-winning greenwood chairs with hide, rush or wicker. Comfortable rocking chairs are well balanced and refuse to let you to slide off. When John's not at the markets, you can find him at 74 Worthing Road, Victoria Point. He's there every market day except Friday night (pictured) actually the best time to go.

Clairvoyants and palm readers seem to have much more of an air of mystery about them in the evening, and there is a wandering calypso band to keep the mood up. Don't be surprised if you bump into a ringtail possum or two, wandering across the path, just checking out the scene. When business gets a bit slow, one of the Murri stallholders busks with his didgeridoo, which adds a lot to the atmosphere. Overall, the markets could do with a lot more food, but it's a good night out. The nervous traveller can have confidence strolling though the markets or the Parklands at night, as they are very well lit. Fri 5pm–10pm; Sat 11am–5pm.

Riverside Markets Saturday 7am–4pm, an excellent market which winds around three levels of the Harry Siedler designed Riverside. City-type eateries are within the building complex and you can find lots of snacks in the stalls, but nothing especially remarkable, except perhaps Fabulous Flat Fruit – all natural – dried and flattened out and also a variety of hand-made crisp savoury snacks.

The bearded guy at the back is getting the instant clay portrait treatment.

It can get crowded, but a good market needs a crowd to keep it alive. This is the market where you'll find a lot of new gear, some beautiful clothes and furniture. **Zofia Mroz** makes clothes, exclusive to Riverside Markets – elegant, eclectic designs for women, though her stuff is so good that one suspects she will be in Milan or New York fairly soon. Just because he looks so good, **Mike Rainer**, tricked out in his chauffeur's uniform and cap, stands guard on Eagle Street with his JFK Harley Davidson offering day trips, tours and joy rides. Aspincade Escorts and Tours.

Indigo Cactus

Indigo Cactus is a little (very little) shop in the Elizabeth Arcade, which runs between Charlotte and Elizabeth streets. All the things in the shop are local products, very arty stuff, in fact some of it pure art with no function at all. Every piece in the shop has the artist's name on the price tag, though you could do with a bit more information on the artist and a bit more room in the shop. As with so much Modern art, it's a bit self-indulgent but they are all one-offs and the stock rotates and you won't catch anyone else wearing it. Jewellery, gifts, clocks, bowls, bags and plenty more, and reasonably priced. Indigo Cactus, shop 14 Elizabeth Street Arcade (99 Elizabeth Street). Fish sculpture on right from Indigo Cactus.

Larrikin

Brigalow and Belah are not well-known timbers, though they are among Australia's hardest and most durable. Using these timbers, John Deshon creates strong, lasting and beautiful furniture for his company **Larrikin Furniture**.

Larrikin chair.

Hardwood refectory tables, are made using 17th century trestle bases and can be custom made for your hall or dining room or even board room up to 10-seater, for less than $1000. The greenwood chairs are the prize, and the best of these are made from felled logs that are cleaved (split), not cut with a saw. The wood is then shaped with a drawknife. The wood is worked while still green as the shrinkage adds to the strength of the chair's joinery. The chairs are then finished with leather, rush or wicker. Rocking chairs are constructed in the same way and are very comfortable and don't try to slide you out. You can find **Larrikin Furniture** at the South Bank markets every Saturday 11am–5pm, or at 74 Worthing Road, Victoria Point.

ENTREPRENEURIAL TRADITION

The goanna was a totem of great spiritual significance for at least two groups of southern Queensland Murries. It had an important part as traditional food and medicine, especially for Northern and Central Australian Aborigines. Goanna or snake fat, sometimes mixed with mud or dirt, was commonly used as a dressing on cuts and wounds. The babies of the Kalkadoon people of north-west Queensland were not washed after birth, but smeared with goanna fat – a practice that

Well, I be Canned.

continued throughout infancy. Goanna fat, particularly the rich deposit from the kidney region, was used to relieve headache and other pain. It was also used as a liniment for tired or aching limbs.

The Brisbane story of the Australian bush remedy Goanna Salve owes as much to Murri traditional medicine as it does to the entrepreneurial flair of an immigrant called Joe Marconi. Joe (real name Mahoney) saw an opportunity and exploited the human desire for quick-fix remedies, creating an irresistible drama around a mixture of goanna oil and native herbs.

Joe Marconi was running a sideshow when he met snake charmer Lyn Vane, who dazzled his audiences with claims of resistance to the deadly venom of his co-workers. As the venom sent him frothing and flailing to the ground, he would rub his "antidote" on the wound and

make a miraculous recovery. Marconi followed Vane into the bush to collect native plants for the ointment and also discovered the Murries' use of liquefied goanna fat as a healing remedy.

Over a period of years, Marconi developed a product combining the penetrating qualities of goanna oil with medicine herbs and plant extracts, including eucalyptus.

Having produced his salve, Marconi used his

shameless showmanship to develop it into a national product highly regarded in both the city and the bush. The great advertising myth was that the product's remarkable penetrating qualities were so great that they could not be contained in a glass bottle.

When the company was sold in 1982, the secret ingredients came to light – Joe hadn't used goanna products since the reptiles had become a protected species. "Goanna" products are still manufactured in Brisbane today by Herron Pharmaceuticals and include the following traditional ingredients: wintergreen oil, eucalyptus oil, camphor, menthol, gum, oils of turpentine, pine and peppermint and gum resin. It still carries the aura of mystique that grew out of Joe Marconi's great showmanship.

Bookshops

Archives, fine books, old and new. This massive collection spans three shops 38, 40-42 Charlotte Street. Open every day. If you can't find what you want, you're just not trying. **Bent Books**, open daily and until 9pm on weekends, has Brisbane's best selection of second-hand books, film scripts and sheet music – Mozart to Zappa, 205A Boundary Street West End. **Books on Brunswick**, 368 Brunswick Street; **Dymocks**, main store, 239 Albert Street;

Straight man from Bent Books.

Emma's Bookshop, 82a Vulture Street, West End. At the **Red Books**, 350a Brunswick Street, there is a selection of modern alternative culture books. Girls and guys in trousers and skirts (respectively) flip through Linda Jaivin's *Confessions Of An S&M Virgin* and like tomes. **Folio Books**, 80 Albert Street (on the corner of Mary Street), has good novels and excellent art and photography titles. **Jazzworks** – Greg Quigley has all the good oil. A

BRISBANE.

comprehensive range of hard-to-get jazz books and impossible-to-get sheet music, 54 Latrobe Terrace. **Heritage Editions** has a huge selection of exquisite prints and, up steep stairs, if you are game, original maps (pictured above) and prints at the Antiquarian Print Gallery. You'll need plenty of time on this one as there is a lot to browse through, Camford Square, Milton.

Mary Ryan – an ever-expanding selection of branches – the best is at 179 Latrobe Terrace, Paddington. An excellent bookshop plus food, coffee and atmosphere in the cafe. The cafe is lined with author posters – most of them signed – and is under the shop looking over a lovely garden path leading to a pagoda. They organise literary club nights in conjunction with the *Courier Mail* . Other branches: Brisbane Arcade (160 Queen Street), and 730 Brunswick Street, New Farm. **Read's Rare Books** if Harri and Mark don't have it, they find it; if they cant find it, it doesn't exist. 40 George Street, Brisbane and Fortitude Valley. **University of Queensland Bookshop**, not just sellers of reference and scholarly books, but fiction, non-fiction and poetry too. Staff House Road, St Lucia campus and also at the Gatton campus. The **Women's Bookshop**, Gladstone Road, Highgate Hill.

A list of recommended books around and about Brisbane, with thanks to University of Queensland Bookshop.

Wild Places of Greater Brisbane and **Wildlife of Greater Brisbane** By Stephen Poole and others, Queensland Museum Publications. Each, $24.95; **Johnno** by David Malouf, published by Pengun;. **Two to the Valley**, by David Hinchcliffe and Dennis Bailey, published by The Valley Business Association; **12 Edmondstone Street**, David Malouf (Penguin) $16.95; **Johnno**, David Malouf (Penguin) $16.95; **Zig Zag Street**, Nick Earls (Transworld) $16.95; *The Mayne Inheritance,* Rosalind Siemon (QUP) $17.95; **Tirra Lirra By The River**, Jessica Anderson (Picador) $16.95; **Praise**, Andrew McGahan (Allen & Unwin) $16.95; **Reminiscences of Early Queensland**, Tom Petrie (UQP) $19.95; **Collected Stories,** Thea Astley (UQP) $17.95; **Collected Stories,** Janet Turner Hospital (UQP) $17.95; **David Malouf Poems 1959–1989** (UQP) $29.95; **Messages from Chaos**, Susan Johnson $12.95; **My People, Ooodgeroo Noonuccal** (Jacaranda Wiley) $18.95, **Steam Pigs**, Melissa Lucashenko, (UQP) $16.95.

12 Things to Know

INCLUDES:

Emergency services and advice; visitors' information; how the transport system works; information on buses, ferries, parking, shuttle services

Compass on your dashboard – an essential navigation tool in Brisbane. Feather optional extra.

	J	F	M	A	M	J	J	A	S	O	N	D
Maximum (C)	29	29	28	27	24	21	21	22	24	26	27	29
Minimum (C)	21	21	20	17	14	11	10	10	13	16	18	20
Rainfall (mm)	169	177	152	86	84	82	66	45	34	102	95	123
Rain days	14	14	15	11	10	8	7	7	7	10	10	11

CLIMATE AND CLOTHING

Brisbane enjoys a sub-tropical climate, with long summers and mild, dry winters. Casual, lightweight clothing is for standard dress and be sure to bring a swimsuit, hat and sunscreen. Something a little warmer (a cardigan or jacket) may be required for winter mornings and evenings. There are 320 sunny days a year in Brisbane and the average temperature is 13°C minimum and 29°C maximum.

GENERAL INFORMATION

• Brisbane is the largest single municipal government in the world, after New York and Los Angeles. It is built on 11 hills, has a land area of 1220 sq km and has a population of 786,442.

• Queensland does not have daylight saving in summer. Be careful of your travel bookings when other Australian states are in daylight saving time.

QUIRKY INFORMATION

• One of the great urban myths of Brisbane is that the money raised to build a new Catholic Cathedral was sent to Rome to be blessed by the Pope and was never returned.

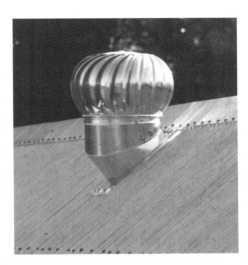

(The cathedral was to have been built on land bounded by Ann, Gipps and Wickham streets). The real story is that Archbiship Duhig ran into credit problems that became worse with the onset of the Depression.

• On footpaths, in chalk you may read "Last chance! HURRY HURRY Get your Lucky Casket now!" Be in it to win it. Queensland's Golden Casket lottery. Queenslanders are the nation's biggest gamblers on instant scratchies and prizes to the value of $4.6 million are still unclaimed. You have seven years to get yours.

GETTING AROUND

For a long time Brisbane gave the impression of being an overgrown country town, sprawling and ungainly as it expanded over hills and dales. With the rediscovery of the Brisbane River, the ugly ducking city is turning into something of a swan, with the snaking band of water binding it together, giving it a coherence as well as providing a central point of reference that makes it more welcoming, knowable, interesting and attractive.

Whenever possible, take the opportunity to

travel via the River. As more development takes place along its banks over the coming years, this form of water transport will get better and better. In the meantime, use the map below to orient and guide you to some of the key places of interest now by the River.

Ferries include the **CityCats**, which operate between Hamilton and The University of Queensland, along with a number of inner-city and cross-river services

CityCat Service

The Cats cruise Brisbane City at least half hourly from 6am daily. Last service leaves Bretts Wharf and the University of Queensland at 10.30pm.

Murri names for CityCat fleet

Murri names for areas along the River were chosen for the CityCat fleet. The first was *Kurilpa*, the area at West End and South Brisbane and then *Tugulawah* after the River area near Bulimba. When later members of the current fleet were introduced they were named: *Barrambin,* (the valley to the north of Breakfast Creek; *Bikinba,* the original name for New Farm point, *Miajin*, Gardens Point and *Mirbarpa,* which is what Indooroopilly was originally called. Indooroopilly, incidentally is Murri for "leech gully".

BICYCLES

Another great gift the Brisbane River has given to its city are the flats along its banks. These have encouraged the building of 350km of bicycle tracks, making for easy travel across the city and enjoyable recreation. The BCC's (Brisbane City Council) "Bicyle Brisbane Plan" includes adding bicycle lanes and the hope is that by 2011 up to 8 percent of all commuter traffic to and from work and school will be bicycles.

Up-to-date bookets on Brisbane bikeways are free and available from libraries, ward offices and Council Customer Service Centres.

Useful telephone numbers

Brisbane City Council, Tel 3403 8888
BCC Bikeway Planning Officer,
Tel 3403 3925
Queensland Cyclist Association,
Tel 3390 1489
Brisbane Touring, Tel 3399 8212
Bicycle Institute of Queensland,
Tel 3844 1144
For information on where to hire bicycles and for more general information and ideas on bicycling, see 7 THINGS TO DO.

Web sites

There are a number of web sites that purport to give information on Brisbane and we checked them out for you.
The Brisbane City Council runs a ripper, full of good stories, community information and local cultural services: **www.brisbane-stories.powerup.com.au**
For a comprehensive list of 14 skate, blade and BMX pipes, walls and tracks: **www.brisbane.qld.gov.au**
But that's about it – the rest is a bit touristy. Our own website for updated information **www.untourist.com.au**

If you need help with the public transport services available in a specific area, call **TransInfo 13 12 30**. Tell them your address

and where you wish to travel and they will provide public transport information to best meet your needs. **Brisbane Transport** operates a number of different bus and ferry services throughout the city, including:

BUSES

CityXpress buses provide a premium limited-stops service. Usually half hourly during the day and more frequently during peak periods.

All Stops Services stop regularly in the city and suburbs.

City Circle (333) buses make getting around the city centre easy. The City Circle buses run every five minutes from 8am–5.30pm weekdays.

Great Circle Line (598/599) connects major suburban shopping centres and links with the majority of CityXpress routes.

City Tours highlight Brisbane attractions with three bus tours:

City Sights tours travel to key historical, cultural and tourist points of interest in and around Brisbane City.

City Heights tours includes a visit to Mt Coot-

Bus and ferry fares are calculated on the number of zone boundaries crossed and in the case of ferries, the number of sectors crossed. **Brisbane Transport** has a wide range of ticketing options. Single tickets can be purchased from your bus or ferry operator, or you can purchase tickets from a number of agencies.

tha lookout and also the City Botanic Gardens. **City Nights** services depart daily and travel to key vantage points (including Mt Coot-tha lookout and a short trip on a CityCat) to take in the sights of Brisbane by night. **Night Rider** operates every 15 minutes on Friday and Saturday nights between 8pm–3pm. The bus route travels around the inner city linking entertainment areas, including Petrie Terrace and Caxton Street, Fortitude Valley, Riverside, the Casino and other city venues.

After 9.30 pm Set Down Passengers who are travelling on services departing the City after 9.30pm are able to alight at any point on the route where it is safe for both the operator and the passenger. Special conditions apply for CityXpress services.

Hail and Ride

444 Highgate Hill (operates daily) Starts at 7am from Boundary Street (outside Caltex Garage) West End then runs approximately every 10 minutes in an anticlockwise direction. The last bus leaves Boundary Street, West end at 7.05pm Monday to Saturday. Can be hailed at any point along the route safely where there is a green line painted on the kerb.

555 New Farm/Teneriffe (operates daily) Starts at 7am from Merthyr Road, New Farm (opposite Coles), then runs about every 15 minutes in an anticlockwise direction. The last bus leaves Merthyr Road at 6.30pm, returning here by 7pm. Due to traffic conditions in Ann Street, Hail and Ride 555 picks up and sets down at selected bus stops. In the New Farm area, the bus will stop anywhere on the route as close as safety allows.

WHERE TO BUY TICKETS

Ticket agents – Tickets are available from ticket agents throughout Brisbane (most ticket agents are newsagents). Keep a lookout for the distinctive gold and white flag at more than 300 locations.

Council Customer Service Centres – These can also provide timetables for local areas. The locations of these centres are as follows:
• 69 Ann Street, Brisbane City;
• Indooroopilly Shopping Town;
• Chermside Shopping Centre;
• Garden Centre Shopping Centre;
• Fortitude Valley, TC Beirne Centre, Brunswick Street Mall;
• Inala Civic Centre;
• Wynnum Administration Centre, Charlotte Street.

Bus and ferry tickets
Ten Trip Saver cards provide 10 single or transfer trips at a discounted price.

Off Peak Savers allow unlimited travel (except on tours/special services) at a huge discount between 9am and 3.30pm and after 7pm weekdays, all day Saturday and Sunday and on public holidays.

Day Rover allows unlimited travel on buses

and ferries (except tour/special buses) for one day. A bus, rail and ferry ticket called Roverlink is also available.

Weekly and Monthly Tickets offer unlimited travel on buses and ferries within the specified zones for seven days or one month from first day of use.

Group savers are sold to adults travelling with children. Valid weekdays between 9am–3.30pm and after 7pm with all-day travel on weekends and public holidays (group discounts are limited to a maximum of two adults, and each group must consist of at least one adult and one child under 15.

Tertiary Tickets (monthly, semester, annual) give discounts to students and are available from Council Customer Service Centres.

TIMETABLES

For a comprehensive range of timetables and brochures on Brisbane Transport bus, ferry and tour services and ticket options, call at any of the following Brisbane Transport Customer Service Locations:

• Garden City Bus Interchange, Upper Mt Gravatt
• Queen Street Mall Kiosk, City;
• Queen Street Bus Station, Lower Level, Myer Centre, City;
• Brisbane Administration Centre, Lower Ground Level, City.

Suburban Customer Service Centres carry a range of brochures and timetables for services in that local area. Your local library and ward offices also carry a limited number of local area timetables.

Council-operated car parks

King George Square Car Park (the entrance is from Roma Street) Tel 3403 4420 Hours of operation: Mon–Thurs 6.30am to midnight; weekends open continuously from 6.30am Fri–11pm Sunday; public holidays, except Christmas Day and Boxing Day, 7.30am–9pm.

Normally closed on Sundays and public holidays except where justified by anticipated demand for extraordinary events.

Wickham Terrace Car Park (the entrances are from Turbot Street and Wickham Terrace) Tel 3403 1323 Hours of operation: Mon to Thurs 6.30am–10.30pm; Mon to Thurs 6.30am to midnight; Friday, 6.30am–midnight; Saturday 8.30am–1.30pm. Normally closed Sundays and public holidays except where justified by anticipated demand for extraordinary events.

ROADS

The Brisbane Metroad System
This map shows, in generalised form, the pattern of roads signposted as METROADS. The new system supersedes existing route numbers on the same roads but unaffected State Routes continue with signposting as at present.

GETTING THERE

Air

Brisbane International Airport (the domestic terminal is alongside) is 15 kilometres from the city centre and more than 20 international airlines provide regular services from ports throughout the world. If you are entering Australia, try to book any domestic flights in advance as internal air travel in Australia is very expensive unless you are booking discounted flights which, for the best value, usually need to be booked well in advance. Retween 6am and 8pm. The fare is less than $10. The taxi fare is around $20; limosines and hire car services are also available.

Self-drive

From Sydney, Brisbane is 1002 kilometres along Highway 1. The inland route follows Highway 1 to Newcastle, then Highway 15, which passes through the New England district of NSW.

To the north of Brisbane are the Glasshouse Mountains and the lush valleys of the Caboolture Shire, plus the beautiful beaches of the Sunshine Coast and Bribie Island. To the east is Moreton Bay, the islands and the bayside districts; and to the west are the fruit and vegetable fields of Gatton, the Darling Downs city of Toowoomba and villages of the early pioneers. The Gold Coast is within easy reach south of the city, as are the farming plains of Beaudesert and the mountain ridges of the Macpherson Ranges and Lamington National Park.

If you want to venture into the surrounding areas, see Chapter 13 OUT OF BRISBANE.

Rail

Long distance services are available from the southern states. In NSW, **CountryLink** operates an overnight **XPT** service beween Sydney and Brisbane (14 hours), Tel (02) 9379 3000. Trains arrive/depart at Central Station in the heart of the city, Ann and Edward streets. **Queensland Rail** operates several modern long distance passenger services from and to Brisbane from stations at Queensland's coastal and inland cities.

Coach

Coach services from interstate and intrastate operate daily into Brisbane's **Transit Centre** in Roma Street, close to the city centre. Most coaches have air conditioning, onboard loos and video. Long-distance bus companies: **Coach Trans**, Tel 3236 1000; **Greyhound Pioneer Australia**, Tel 3258 1670,

Reservations 13 20 30, Freecall 1800 801 294; **McCafferty's**, Reservations, 13 14 99.

THE CITY

The CBD of Brisbane is compact, making it easy to explore on foot. An extensive network of modern public transport facilities can get you to sights, attractions, hotels and transport terminals.

For useful information on Brisbane, including a **Calendar of Events,** a fast-facts page, maps and transport information, see the front pages of the A-K volume of the **Yellow Pages** Brisbane telephone directory.

TOURIST OFFICES

Queen Street Mall Information Centre, corner Queen and Albert Streets, Monday to Thursday, 9am–5.30pm, Friday 9am–9pm, Saturday 9am–4pm and Sunday 10am–4pm, Tel: 3229 5918. There is a small 24 hour police station at the centre.

Transit Centre Information Office (Level 2, Roma Street Transit Centre) is run by the Greater Brisbane Tourist Association. Open weekdays 8am–6pm; weekends 9am–1pm. Tel 3236 2020.

Brisbane Tourism runs an information desk at City Hall on King George Square, weekdays 9am–4.30pm; Saturday 10am–1pm Tel 3221 8411.

Conventions – all convention information (venues, organisers etc) is through

Brisbane Tourism, Tel 3221 8411.

The Brisbane City Council has a number of **touch-screen terminals** in its **InfoBrisbane** information booths around town.

Money change

Money can be changed at Brisbane International Airport. Thomas Cook has three foreign exchange offices in the city, Level E of the Myer Centre, corner Elizabeth and Albert Streets at the top of the escalators, open weekdays 8.45am–5.15pm; Saturday 9.30 am–1pm. Also at 276 Edward St, and the first floor at 241 Adelaide St (opposite Qantas' international office). American Express is at 131 Elizabeth St, near the Albert Street corner Tel 3229 2729.

Left Luggage

In the Brisbane airport, there are lockers for left-luggage.
In the Transit Centre on Roma St, there are large, backpack-size lockers up on the 3rd level.

Post and Telecommunications

Brisbane's major post office, the GPO, open weekdays 9am to 5pm, is an imposing Victorian building on Queen Street, between Edward and Creek streets. The *poste restante* section is just inside the front door on the left-hand side.

There's another post office on level 2 of the Myer Centre in the Queen Street Mall and it is open on weekends.

The **STD** telephone area code within Australia for Brisbane is 07. Overseas callers, omit "0".

Consulates
Austria – 20 Argyle Street, Breakfast Creek (Tel 3262 8955)
Denmark – 180 Queen Street, City (Tel 3221 8641)
France – 10 Market Street, City (Tel 3229 8201)
Germany – 10 Eagle Street, City (Tel 3221 7819)
Greece – 215 Adelaide Street, City (Tel 3229 5677)
Italy – 133 Leichhardt Street, Spring Hill (Tel 3832 0099)
Japan –12 Creek Street, City (Tel 3221 5188)
Netherlands – 101 Wickham Terrace, City (Tel 3839 9644)
New Zealand – 288 Edward Street, City (Tel 3221 9933)
Norway – 301 Wickham Terrace, Fortitude Valley (Tel 3854 1855)
Spain – 131 Elizabeth Street, City (Tel 3221 8571)
Sweden – 60 Edward Street, City (Tel 3221 9797)
Thailand – 101 Wickham Terrace, Spring Hill, (Tel 3832 1999)
UK – BP House, 193 North Quay, City (Tel 3236 2575)
USA – 383 Wickham Tce, Spring Hill, (Tel 831 3330)

Useful Organisations
The Royal Automobile Club of Queensland (**RACQ**) (Tel 3361 2444) has an office beside the GPO at 261 Queen Street. Good maps on Queensland and an accommodation booking service, plus a while-you-wait passport photo service.

Queensland's **Department of Environment & Heritage** has an information centre called **Naturally Queensland** at 160 Ann Street. Open weekdays, 8.30am–5pm. Maps, brochures and books on Queensland's national parks and state forests here, plus a good range of posters, maps, books and souvenirs relating to conservation and the environment, Tel 3227 8186.

Queensland Government Travel Centre, Cnr Adelaide and Edward streets, City, Tel 13 1801.

Gay and Lesbian
Yearly events: Gay Pride Fest, June/July; Jiembra Fest, around October
Gay run/friendly restaurants/cafes: Gerties, New Farm; Espressohead, West End; Bitch Cafe, Fortitute Valley; Moray Cafe, is at New Farm.
Bookshops: Bent Books; Brooks on Brunswick; Women's Bookshop (Detail, 11 BEST THINGS TO BUY).
Newspapers: *Queensland Pride, Brother Sister Queensland.*
Radio: 4ZZZ (102.2FM), *Dykes on Mikes* every second Wednesday.

Health Service: 38 Gladstone Road, Highgate Hill, Tel 3844 6806.
Queensland Aids Council, 32 Peel Street, Tel 3844 1990.

DISABLED

The Brisbane City Council runs a **Disability Services Unit** Tel 3224 8031 but, be mindful, it is sometimes closed on major holidays. However, a useful forwarding telephone number will be given.

The Council's *Brisbane Disability Map* provides comprehensive disability information, plus map, on the CBD and a map of Mt Coot-tha Botanic Gardens. The map includes futher details and telephone numbers on resources available.

BOOKSHOPS

Large book chains

Dymocks has several city shops including 235 Albert Street; **Angus & Robertson Bookworld**, has three city shops, including one in Post Office Square in Adelaide Street. **Independent booksellers** (see 11 BEST THINGS TO BUY)

Maps

Travelog, Sunmap and UBD all publish Brisbane city and suburban maps that are available from most bookshops and newsagencies for around $5. World Wide Maps & Guides, 239 George Street (between Queen and Adelaide streets) for everything to do with maps and travel and language guides.

Newspapers and Magazines

Brisbane's daily newspaper is *The Courier Mail.* There is also a Brisbane edition of the national newspaper, *The Australian.* There are also a lot of local entertainment magazines.

TV

Brisbane has five TV channels, one, ABC-TV, is government funded and has no commercials; SBS, a UHF channel, has excellent multicultural programs and a top international news service.

Radio

Brisbane has an excellent alternative music station, 4ZZZ (102.1FM). The Murri contry station is 4AAA (98.9) The national ABC (no commercials) stations are 4RN, 792AM; 4QR, 612AM and classic FM is on 106.1FM. JJJ is the ABC's youth network with its alternative and independent music (107.7FM).

Film and Photography

Camera Tech, 127 Creek Street, is the repair agent for Canon and Konica, and attends to other makes as well.

SOME BRISBANE CITY COUNCIL FACILITIES

Sports available at BCC facilities:

For fun, fitness, competition and entertainment, there's lots going on at the Sleeman Sports Complex and Chandler –

aerobics, badminton, gymnastics, netball swimming. Address: Cnr Old Cleveland and Tiley Roads, Tel 3245 8011.

Skateboarding

There are 17 skateboarding facilities across Brisbane. For information, Tel 3403 6757.

Swimming Pools

Of Brisbane's 18 public swimming pools, five are heated and open all year (Fortitude Valley, Yeronga, Sleeman Sports Complex, Centenary and Chermside). The remainder are open from September to April: Bellbowrie, Jindalee, Langlands Park and Sandgate also provide small heated teaching pools. Some of the facilities and services provided by Brisbane City Pools include hydrotherapy pools, water slides, river rides, indoor sports centres, gymnasiums, coffee lounges and refreshment kiosks a well as an abundance of shade structures.

There are three months of the Brisbane year that are usually just too hot. If a swim is the thing, then here is a list of the pools, so pick the closest one and just add water.

Arcadia Ridge 131 Beaudesert Rd (near Mannington Rd in Clair O'Sullivan Park)
Bellbowrie Sugarwood Street (opposite Goast Gum Street), Tel 3202 6620
Carole Park corner Boundary and Waterford streets, Tel 3271 4540
Chernside 375 Hamilton Road (oppisite Eastly St), Tel 3356 6134
Chandler Aquatic Center (Sleeman Sports complex) Corner Old Cleveland and Tilly Roads, Tel 3403 9635
City (Centenary pool) 400 Gregory Terrace (opposite Park Street, Spring Hill), Tel 3821 8259
City (Spring Hill Baths) 14 Torrington Street, Spring Hill, Tel 3831 7881
Corinda (Dunlop Park pool) 794 Oxley Road (opposite Allen Terrace in Dunlop Park), Tel 3379 1630
Fortitude Valley (Valley Pool) Corner Wickham Street and East Street, Tel 3852 7881
Greenslopes (Langlands Park pool) 5 Panitya Street (near Old Cleveland Road in Langlands Park, Tel 3397 1231
Jindalee Corner Yallambee Road and Looranah Street, Tel 3376 1002
Manly Pool 1 Fairlead Crescent Manly, Tel 3396 3281
Newmarket Corner Alderson Sreett and Enoggera Road Sedgley Park, Tel 3356 8434
Paddington (Ithaca Pool) 131 Caxton Street (near Hale St), Tel 3369 2624
Sandgate 231 Flinders Pde (opposite 8th Avenue), Tel 3269 7946
South Brisbane (Musgrave Park Pool) 100 Edmonstone Street (opposite Besant Street in Musgrave Park), Tel 3844 3858
Toowong Corner Coronation Drive and Booth Street, Tel 3870 0270
Upper Mount Gravat (Hibiscus Gardens pool) 98 Klump Road (opposite Timor Street), Tel 3349 8836
Yeronga 81 School Road (oposite Albemarle Street in Yeronga Park), Tel 3848 8575

City Botanic Gardens Mangrove Walk

The mangrove boardwalk at the Gardens runs for 380 metres and allows visitors to walk to the Brisbane River. Walkers can see a wide variety of birds, and environmental features are marked by signage along the walk.

Brisbane Botanic Gardens

Free guided walks, Tel 3229 1554
Cafe bookings, Tel 3229 1554

Mt Coot-tha Aboriginal Plant and Art Trails

Visitors to the Brisbane Botanic Gardens at Mt Cooth-tha can learn via a self-guided trail how traditional and contemporary Murri groups made use of the Australian rainforest plants for food, medicine, shelter, utensils and tools. Located near J C Slaughter-Falls is the Aboriginal Art Trail. Its aim is to combine art and appreciation of Murri culture with the pleasures of walking in the bush. The 1.5 kilometre track features tree carvings, rock paintings, etchings, rock arrangements and a dance pit.

Natural areas

BCC has preserved a number of Natural Areas that are worth a visit

Tinchi Tamba Wetlands, Bald Hills. Picnic facilities, boat launch, walking tracks.
Toohey Forest, Nathan, Mt Gravatt and Moorooka. Open forest – picnic facilities, walking tracks.

Karawatha Forest, Karawatha. Open forest and wetlands – picnic facilities, walking tracks.

Boondall Wetlands, Boondall. Wetlands – picnic facilities, walking tracks, bikeways, bird hides, canoe launch.

Bayside Parklands, Wynnum, Manly, Lota and Gumdale. A series of parks, including mangroves, open forest and the foreshore.

Mt Coot-tha Forest Park. Walking tracks and picnic facilities. Park headquarters, Tel 3300 4855.

Other BCC Parks Information

North, Tel 3403 7170
South, Tel 3404 5649
East, Tel 3403 5438
West, Tel 3403 2552

Civic Entertainment Program

The Council provides a regular program of free daytime and early evening concerts at City Hall, city parks and some suburban venues. The program includes classical and chamber music, jazz and brass band and military concerts, world music and light entertainment, Tel 3403 8888.

MEDICAL SERVICES

The Travellers' Medical & Vaccination Centre. at 245 Albert Street. Open weekdays

8.30am–5pm (Wednesday until 6 pm) and on Saturday, 8.30am–1.30pm, Tel 3221 3611.

Medical clinics include the **Traveller's Medical Service** 5th floor Coles building, 210 Queen Street in the mall, Tel 3221 8083

The **Brisbane Sexual Health Clinic**, 484 Adelaide Street, open Monday, Tuesday, Thursday and Friday 9a,–5pm and on Wednesday 9am to noon, Tel 3227 8666.

The **Gay and Lesbian Welfare Association**, Tel 3839 3277

Chemists open late include the T&G Corner Pharmacy, at 141 Queen St in the Mall, (Mon–Sat 8am–9pm, Sunday 10am–5pm) and the Transit Centre Pharmacy in Roma Street (open weekdays 7am–6pm and Saturday 7am–1.30pm).

EMERGENCIES

Dial Tel 000 for emergency help from the police, ambulance or fire brigade. There's a 24-hour police station in the centre of the city in the Queen Street Mall Information Centre, Tel 3220 0752 for emergency assistance, call Tel 3364 6464.

Rape/Incest Crisis Centre, Tel 3844 4008
Life-Line Counselling Service (24 hours), Tel 13 77 14
Women's Infolink counselling service, Tel 3229 1580 or Freecall 1800 177 577
Youth Emergency Services Inc, Tel 3357 7655

Salvo Careline (Salvation Army), Tel 1300 363 622
Interpreter Service (24 hours), 100 Edward Street, Tel 13 14 50

HOSPITALS

In the event of an accident or emergency, you can go to the Accident and Emergency Department of the hospitals listed. Accident and Emergency Departments are open 24 hours a day, seven days a week.

Royal Brisbane Hospital, Herston Road, Herston 4006 Tel 3253 8111
Royal Children's Hospital, Herston Road, Herston 4006, Tel 3253 3777
Mater Misericordiae Hospital, Raymond Terrace, South Brisbane 4104, Tel 3840 8111
Princess Alexandra Hospital, Ipswich Road, Woolloongabba 4102, Tel 3240 2111
Prince Charles Hospital, Rode Road, Chermside 4032, Tel 3350 8111
Queen Elizabeth II Jubilee Hospital, Kessels Road, Coopers Plains 4108, Tel 3275 6111

DENTAL HOSPITALS

Dental Hospital (Brisbane), Turbot Street (Cnr Albert Street) Brisbane 4000, Tel 3231 3777
Dental Hospital (Children's), Herston Road, Herston 4006, Tel 3253 1025
South Brisbane Dental Hospital, Main Street, Woolloongabba, 4102 Tel 3391 3754

ANNUAL EVENTS

January 26
Australia Day Celebrations, Australia's national day, various city-wide activities.

Early April
Brisbane to Gladstone Yacht Race & Festival. A tradition, now half a century old, includes yacht race, festival and exhibition of memorabilia. For more information, Tel 3265 3492

Early May
Queensland Jazz Carnival. Showcasing Queensland jazz musicians includes river cruise, big band ball and workshops. Tel 3265 7711

May - June
Queensland Winter Racing Carnival. This is the main horse-racing season.

End of May
Paniyiri Greek Festival. Celebration of Greek customs and culture, dances and cuisine. Tel 3844 1166

June 6
Queensland's special day is the focus of a week of activities, Tel 3358 1500

July-August
Brisbane International Film Festival. A showcase of Australian and international feature, short, animated and documentary films. Tel 3220 0444

Mid-August
"The Ekka" – Royal Brisbane Show. Brisbane's famous Royal National Agriculture Show, a combination of culture and carnivale, trade and agricultural exhibitions and events. Tel 3852 1831

August-September
Brisbane Festival has been held biennially, but may soon be held annually. At the Queensland performing Arts Complex and various other locations. Tel 3840 7444

Early September
Spring Hill Fair – one of Brisbane's most popular annual local festivals. held in Water Street, spring Hill, with market stalls, food and entertainment. Tel 3831 5591.

September-October
Brisbane River Festival. For information, Tel 3403 8888

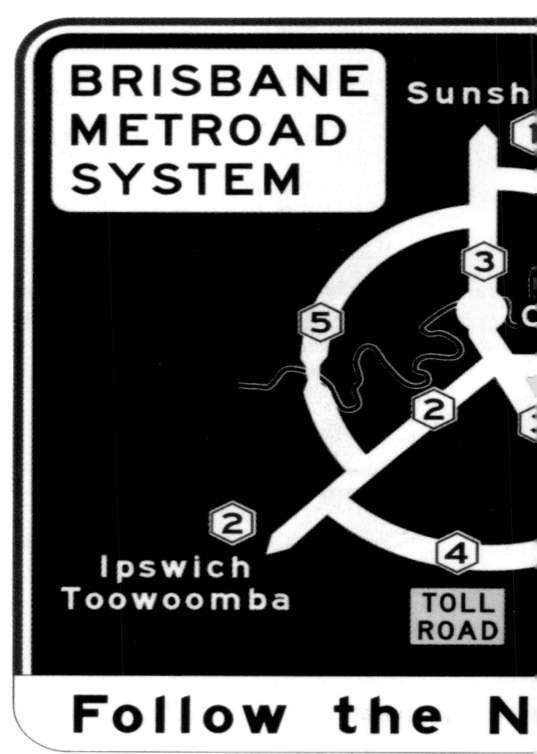

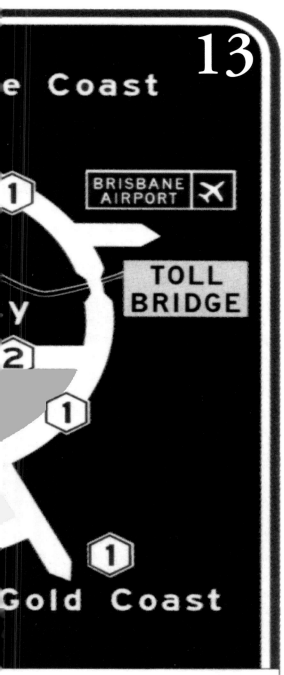

13 Out of Brisbane

INCLUDES: *The pick of day trips out of Brisbane, the locals favourite short breaks including the Sunshine Coast, the off-shore islands, the Darling Downs and the hinterlands.*

I f you take a map of south-east Queensland and trace a circle about 100 kilometres from the centre of the city, you can see why Brisbane is one of the great unsung holiday hubs in Australia. Within an hour or so's drive from the centre of Brisbane are some of the best untourist (and, true, tourist) playgrounds in Australia. People who live in Brisbane are the first to agree – it's one of the best things about the city and why they like living there.

However, for people visiting Queensland, Brisbane is often considered a place you pass through on the way to somewhere else. An hour's drive to the south you'll find the Gold Coast, although not our choice of an untourist place to visit. Inland and still within easy reach of Brisbane are hinterlands that have marvellous, unspoiled areas and great places to stay. To the north is the Sunshine Coast – stylish, understated and with its great locally grown produce, it's everything the Gold Coast isn't. Then west to the wonderful expanse of the Darling Downs – the bread basket of the state. And to the east the getaway of North Stradbroke Island.

In this chapter we will pick the best bits out of these many jewels. If you want more detail and to seriously study the best places to stay in south-east Queensland, then the publication *Untourist Queensland* is for you.

Gold Coast

To the untrained eye there is not a whole lot for the untourist in Surfers Paradise on the Gold Coast. To the trained eye there still isn't a lot for the untourist in Surfers Paradise – unless the traveller is under one and a half metres tall, in which case he/she would probably be in heaven. A new theme park every day, bungie jumping, helicopter and seaplane joy flights, casinos with mono-rails, chair lifts to a magic castle, mini golf, cable skiing, sky diving, ballooning. After all, Surfers was developed for the fully-fledged card-carrying tourist, complete with Miami-style hotel/motels, gold bikini-clad meter maids and Japanese street signs. The council has only recently started to remove these signs as the Japanese complained their holiday experience was not complete if they couldn't get lost, and as every good untourist knows, it's important to find the unexpected. Most of the "attractions" are in your face, so you don't need even to go looking for them.

GETTING THERE: Leave the city on the South West Freeway (Route 3) and on to the Pacific Highway (Route 1)

Local recommendation

"I take Highway 1 and avoid getting to the Gold Coast by turning off at Sanctuary Cove for Tamborine Mountain. I head for the Lamington National Park," says Janie Hampton, who picks this as her favourite weekend stop. " I love it because the forest is overwhelmingly ancient and fascinating. I've often described it to my friends as the Barrier Reef of forests."

Romeo Lahey (left), a Lamington pioneer.

Lamington National Park

The Lamington National Park is the most spectacular, most visited National Park on the east coast, with ancient beech forest and a rugged landscape that reflects the character of the people who settled it. In 1911, a bunch of blokes from an Irish family named O'Reilly trekked 1000 kilometres north from the Blue Mountains west of Sydney to the Macpherson Range, and claimed 100 acres of prime sub-tropical rainforest on Green Mountain. As soon as a track was constructed, visitors (who travelled two days by horseback from Brisbane), were attracted by the evolutionary, rugged beauty of the mountain and the O'Reilly boys would put them up in the family slab hut. As the numbers grew, a decision was made to give up the cows and build a guesthouse farther up the hill. The doors to **O'Reilly's** where first opened at Easter, 1926, and the family has been welcoming guests ever since then.

The road that now links this guesthouse with the world was built in the early '30s by another family concern, Lahey Limited. Romeo Lahey and Arthur Groom started construction on another guesthouse, **Binna Burra**, just outside the boundary of the national park but still surrounded by luscious forest. Binna Burra opened its doors in 1933.

These two fine guesthouses opened up the area for day trips and they can be also be used as service stops to roam the forest. Binna Burra also has a beautiful camping area.

GETTING THERE: Out of town on the South West Freeway (Route 3) and on to the Pacific Highway (Route 1) turn off at Beenleigh on to the Beaudesert - Beenleigh Rd and on though Tamborine and Canungra.

The Natural Bridge

The Springbrook National Park, one and a half hours south of Brisbane is mostly inaccessible and rugged. Only two features are easy to get to. One is the **Best of All lookout** and from here you can see a beautiful view of Byron Bay and Murwillumbah. Before you get to the lookout you will come across a little section of exquisite forest that reminds you of the Lamington National Park, with Antarctic beech trees reaching for the sky. The real attraction up here is the **Natural Bridge** (sometimes refereed to as Natural Arch) carved out of the rock over thousands of years by Cave Creek. Here are the best places to see glowworms and the best time to see them is at night after rain. That sounds like fun, in the dark, in the rain, in the bush. Fear not, the Bridge is surprisingly close to the car park but don't think the worms will light your way because they live in the cave. Take a torch.

GETTING THERE: Out of town on the South West Freeway (Route 3) and on to the Pacific Highway (Route 1) and turn off just after the Nerang River on to Gilston Road, then Latimers Crossing, then left into the Nerang - Murwillumbah Road and follow the signs. During the summmer months, this place gets very busy.

Tamborine Mountain

This area, an hour out of Brisbane, has 10 little national parks, a state forest and the **Cedar Creek Environmental Park** at north Tamborine plus some of the best walking tracks and picnic areas anywhere. The towns of North Tamborine and Eagle Heights have good antiques stores to fossick around in as well as some good coffee shops. The **Mud Brick** and the **Bark Hut** are two of the coffee shops – can you see a pattern in the names? Yes, it is a bit hippiesville, but as all those northern NSW towns turned trendy, hippies moved back to Queensland. There are waterfalls in almost all the parks. Cameron Falls in the north-west park is a beautiful place to stop and cool off.

GETTING THERE: Drive out of Brisbane on the South East Freeway (Route 3) and turn off on to the Oxenford - Tamborine Road after the new double bridges at Coomera and just after Dreamworld.

Tourism hard-sell pioneer.

Sunshine Coast

When heading for the Sunshine Coast one option is to take the turn-off to the Bruce Highway which takes you to the **Glass House Mountains.**

Just 60 odd kilometres north of Brisbane you'll come across the mountains that dominate the landscape from Brisbane to the Sunshine Coast. Rising straight up are 10 volcanic plugs, some more then 500 metres above sea level. There are great views from some of the walks. The Glass House Mountains have special significance with the local Murries and you would be wise to stick to the beaten tracks.

Noosa.

Noosa

Noosa, which is on the outer rim of our 100 kilometre easy-access radius from Brisbane, has so much to offer you'll have to check out *Untourist Queensland* for everything you could ever possibly need to know on things to do, see, buy and places to stay in the area. In the meantime, get a taste for the Sunshine Coast hinterland by heading north from Brisbane, via the Glass House Mountains and have a look at some of the great spots in the **Blackall Range**. Formed by ancient basaltic lava flows, the rich red soils of the Range are now covered by a patchwork of rolling green pastures and dense rainforest. With the arrival of the timbergetters, dairy farmers and fruitgrowers, much of the original forest was cleared for settlement in the small towns along the crest of the range – **Maleny, Montville, Flaxton** and **Mapleton.**

Noosa.

Heading north on Route 1, after taking the turnoff for the Glass House Mountains, continue on to Beerwah and head through Landsborough to Maleny, which has a mix of rural life, commerce, the arts and co-operative ventures. There are good arts and crafts galleries and the Sunday Handcraft Market.

More Noosa.

From Maleny, head for **Kenilworth** on the road that travels along the escarpment for a stunning panoramic view of the Pacific Ocean, the beaches and towns of the Coastal Plain. Kenilworth is such a tiny village that when you stand in the centre of town you can see and feel the open countryside around you. Check out the superb **Lasting Impressions Gallery** there run by Kaye Cathro – it has some first-class Queensland art works. Open 10am–5pm daily. You can head on to **Eumundi** from here, but if it's the weekend you'll be too late for the markets, which we found a bit ho-hum anyway. The township is worth stopping at for afternoon tea at **Eats**. After Eumundi, you can head back to Brisbane on Route 1. The above is only a sketch of what's worth seeing in this area, so in case you have followed your nose and spent longer away from Brisbane than you meant to, you could try **Taylor's Damn Fine Bed and Breakfast** at Eumundi for some overnight shuteye.

Darling Downs

Known as the breadbasket of Queensland, the Darling Downs west of Brisbane is rich, fertile and beautiful to travel through for both landscape and the chance to see traditional small towns. If you plan to stay over, we recommend the wonderful **Argyle Homestead,** a charming old Queenslander, between Gatton and Toowoomba. Tea on the verandah and the big wooden kitchen table is always loaded with fresh local produce. At night, stroll down the road for an evening at the local pub. Great stuff. For day trips, probably the farthest you should go is to Allora, via Toowoomba.   Nearby Nobby has Rudd's Pub where author Steele Rudd created those fabled Australian characters Dad and Dave. This is where you should stop for a beer and a story recital.

Toowoomba is called the garden city and it doesn't take very long to figure out why. Everything is neat and rich and flowering. At **Greenridge Botanicals**, 17 Freighter Avenue, you can do a quick course on herbs both culinary and medicinal as well as have a very healthy snack. The **Weis Restaurant,** 2 Margaret Street, on the other hand, is more your "eat 'till you drop". Bavarian style family lunch place, which is a regular for Brisbane day trippers. Another branch of the same Toowoomba family makes Weis ice blocks, famous all over Australia. There is a very strong German influence in Toowoomba derived from the first immigrants who settled in the Lockyer Valley in the early 1800s. That is beautifully displayed in the Cobb & Co Museum at 27 Lindsay Street, which is probably one of the finest museums of its type in Australia. The Mary Ryan bookshop-cum-cafe is not a bad start if you want to get the insider information on Toowoomba or, better still, get hold of a copy of *Untourist Queensland.*

GETTING THERE: Take Route 54 from Brisbane, through Ipswich and Gatton to Toowoomba. At Toowoomba, take Route 42 to Allora. You can either return on the same highways, or continue south along Route 42 for about 20 kilometres and turn left into Route 15 which takes you back to Route 54 and Brisbane.

Lots of cows.

North Stradbroke, Moreton and Bribie Islands

These islands form Moreton Bay – without them it would be a just a coastal depression with great surf beaches. As a result of their isolation, they have developed unique variations on species and fauna. Freshwater lakes sit within the sand-covered water table, supporting all the links in the chain. Bribie Island, unlike Moreton or North Stradbroke, is flat as a pancake and connected to the mainland by the Caboolture-Bribie Island Road Bridge, about an hour from Brisbane. This island holds more bird and plant life species than either of the other bigger

Waitin' for the Straddie barge.

islands. You enter Bribie through the southern residential area. Moreton Island has many diverse features – rainforest growing straight out of the sand; salt flats covered in little blue soldier crabs; the highest sand dune in the world; lagoons and many more features. **Cape Moreton**, the rock that the sand island formed around, is a good whale-watching spot. One of the Brisbane television stations has a live "whale watch" segment in the news broadcast in April and October. Moreton offers fantastic company, but it's BYO everything. Access via **Combie Trader Barge** from Redcliffe.

North Stradbroke Island also has residents and services to match. We're focussing here on Straddie (as it's called in Brisbane. Stradbroke residents say "the island") because it has samples of all the above island features, good facilities and some excellent accommodation. Some fine, classic Queenslanders can be rented very reasonably – call Ray White Real Estate at Point Lookout, or Dolfin Real Estate, also at Point Lookout.

The welcome waggon when you arrive on North Stradbroke Island claims "best ice-cream ever". Maybe.

NORTH STRADBROKE ISLAND
By Aunty Margaret (Margaret Iselin)

North Stradbroke Island is a beautiful place. Growing up here was a very happy experience, even through we didn't have much. North Stradbroke Island has a rich Aboriginal history. On the foreshore at Polka Point along the Goompi Trail is one of many midden heaps. There are middens right through the Cleveland area and on Peel and Coochiemudlo Islands.

Hundreds of years ago, our people used to make a form of Aboriginal bread called johnny cakes. The bread was originally made from bunya nuts, mixed with water and cooked on the coals. The root from the bungwal fern has a floury core and was also dug up and used to make bread. The Aboriginal people used to canoe down the coast and bring back bunya nuts to the island, and that is why we have them on Stradbroke today.

I am now President of the Aboriginal Elders on the island, and we have formed an organisation called the Minjerribah/Moorgumpin Elders. Minjerribah is the Aboriginal name for North Stradbroke Island and means "island in the sun". Moorgumpin is the Aboriginal name for Moreton Island and means "large sand hill".

We are currently in the process of doing cultural talks and have spoken to 2250 students over the past year. A group of young Aboriginal people, descendants of the Nunukul tribe, form the Yulu-Burri-Ba Dance Troupe. Yulu-Burri-Ba have provided both entertainment and

Brown Lake disguised as blue lake.

cultural education locally and overseas. I believe we have to be here for our young people and education is the best path toward reconciliation.

Above all, we are proud of our island and all the rich heritage and natural wonders North Stradbroke Island has to offer.

For how to get in touch with Margaret and for more information, call Redlands Tourism, Tel 3821 0057.

GETTING THERE: It takes two hours to get to Stradbroke by the vehicular ferry, departing daily from Toondah Harbour, Cleveland. Bookings and enquiries, Tel 3286 2666. You will need to be a good walker if don't take your car. For water transport from Redland Bay, enquiries Tel 3829 0008.

Boaties' Adventures In Paradise

Cruising the coast of Queensland with its islands, reefs and kilometres of untouched sandy beaches is the dream of anyone who ever fancies taking a sailing boat to sea. Bill and Sue Mansill have spent the past 14 years covering these romantic and beautiful waters and they know all the insider spots from Cooktown to the Gold Coast. Their special report is a feature in the book *Untourist Queensland.* Here is what they have to say about Brisbane, the Gold Coast and Noosa:

Brisbane

A buzz day in Brisbane for foot slogging boaties. Tie up at Dockside Marina, Kangaroo Point (call ahead for a berth booking, see Directory). Join the joggers or walk to South Bank following the River. Indulge in coffee and very evil cake. Walk on to Queensland Museum and Queensland Art Gallery, more coffee, cake and culture. Foot or ferry over bridge to CBD and Chinatown in the Valley. Pick up a Peking Duck (around $16), catch a ferry back to Dockside. Bon appetite. Marina guests have free use of hot spa an swimming pool. A fee gives you use of the sports club.

Gold Coast

Sail the Broadwater on Ken Harland's catamaran Coral Sea:. Cruise the **Coomera River**, take in **Sanctuary Cove** for a stop and a shop or lunch. sail south to **Stradbroke Island**, visiting spots like Tippler's Resort for a drink and a swim poolside. Or find a secluded anchorage. Fish, crab, swim, walk the

Prime Time Gold Coast.

beaches and dunes observing wildlife. Picnic on the surfside. For a different view link up with the seaplane and take a scenic flight. You can set the venue and the pace. Ken's Coral Sea in Hope Harbour is available for bookings, minimum of 4. See Directory under Coral Sea.

Even more Noosa.

Noosa

Fabulous Noosa, even more fabulous when you visit by boat. The coastguard will advise on life aboard anchoring restrictions. Our favourite activities are the obligatory morning walk along the tumbleweed track, followed by coffee and croissant at Noosa Surf Life Saving Club – great views of the beach and its pilgrims. Then boogy board the waves at Laguna Bay (or surf Sunshine Beach for the more spirited). Rejoin the boat safely anchored in the Noosa River. Tinnies and houseboats can be hired along the river. Explore Noosa's lake and everglades. Life doesn't end at Hastings Street.

Bill and Sue Mansill

INDEX

DIRECTORY

AREA CODE FOR BRISBANE WHEN CALLING OUTSIDE BRISBANE IS 07 OVERSEAS CALLERS OMIT "0"

Aix Bistro, 83 Merthyr Road, New Farm,Tel 3358 6444

American Express, 131 Elizabeth St, near Albert Street corner, Tel 3229 2729

Anna Yen, Tel 3846 1651

Annie's Shandon Inn, 405 Upper Edward Street, Q 4000,Tel 3831 8684

Archives 38, 40-42 Charlotte Street, Tel 3221 0491
www.archives-bks.com.au/comm/archives

ArgyleHomestead, Tel 4696 6301

Arrivederci Pizza al Metro, 1 Park Road Milton, Tel 3369 8500

Aspincade Escorts and Tours
Tel 015 119 365

Aussie Way Backpackers, 34 Cricket Street, Brisbane Q 4000, Tel 3369 0711

Australian National, Cnr Wellington Street, Woolloongabba, Q4102, Tel 3391 3964

Baguette Restaurant, 150 Racecourse Road, Ascot, Tel 3268 6168

Bardon Fine Foods, 72 MacGregor Terrace, Tel 3369 4766

BCC Parks Information
North, Tel 3403 7170
South, Tel 3404 5649
East, Tel 3403 5438
West, Tel 3403 2552

Bellas Gallery, Cnr James and Robertson Streets,Tel 3257 1608

Bent Books, 205A Boundary Street, West End, Tel 3846 5004

Bicycle Institute of Queensland Inc, PO Box 8321, Woolloongabba, Q 4102

Tel 3844 1144

Bikeway Planning Officer, Tel 3403 3925

Binna Burra, Tel 5533 3622

BIQ,, Tel 3844 1144

Bistrot One, 561 Brunswick Street, New Farm, Tel 3358 3600

Blue Water, Point Lookout, North Stradbroke Island, Tel 3409 8300

Boab, 486 Brunswick Street,Tel 3358 1337

Books on Brunswick, 368 Brunswick Street, Tel 3216 1430

Breakfast Creek Hotel, 2 Kingsford Smith Drive, Breakfast Creek,Tel 3262 5988

Brisbane Bicycle Hire, 87 Albert St Brisbane Tel 3229 2433

Brisbane Botanic Gardens, Alice Street, Tel 3403 7913

Brisbane Botanic Gardens – cafe, see City Gardens Cafe

Brisbane City Council information department, Tel 3403 6757

Brisbane City Council, 69 Ann Street, Tel 3403 888

Brisbane Golf Club, Tennyson Memorial Ave, Yeerongpilly Tel 3848 1008

Brisbane Jazz Club, 1 Annie Street, Kangaroo Point, Tel 3391 2006

Brisbane Sexual Health Clinic, 484 Adelaide Street, Tel 3227 8666

Brisbane Touring Association, Tel 3399 8212

Brisbane Tourism City Hall on King George Square, Tel 3221 8411

Brisbane Visitors & Conventions Bureau, (see Brisbane Tourism)

Browsing On Browning, 11 Browning Street, South Brisbane Tel 3844 0688

Cafe Citrus, 161 Oxford Street, Bulimba, Tel 3899 0242

Cafe Nero, 1 Park Road, Milton, Tel 3369 8400

California Cafe 376 Brunswick Street, Fortitude Valley, Tel 3852 1026

Camera Tech, 127 Creek Street, Tel 3229 5406

Car Parks: King George Square Car Park (the entrance is from Roma Street) Tel 3403 4420; Wickham Terrace Car Park (the entrances are from Turbot Street and Wickham Terrace) Tel 3403 1323

Central Brunswick,455 Brunswick Street, Fortitude Valley, Tel 3852 1411

Cha Cha Char, Eagle Steet Pier, 1 Eagle Street, City, Tel 3211 9944

Chez Laila, Boardwalk, South Bank (Maritime Museum end),Tel 3846 3402

Chez Laila, Boardwalk, South Bank, Tel 3846 3402

City Gardens Cafe, City Botanic Gardens, Alice and George streets (Best entrance via Gardens Point Road), Tel 3229 1554

Civic Entertainment Program, Tel 3403 8888.

Coach Trans, Tel 3236 1000; Greyhound Pioneer Australia, Tel 3258 1670, Reservations,13 20 30, Freecall 1800 801 294; McCafferty's, Reservations, 13 14 99

Conrad Treasury Hotel Casino, William and George Streets, City, Tel 3306 8888

Contemporary Art and Design Vallery, 33 Logan Road, Woolloongabba Tel 3392 0033

Contemporary Furniture Studio, 16 Logan Road, Woolloongabba, Tel 3391 5788

Continental Cafe, 21 Barker Street, New Farm, Tel 3254 0377

Conventions, see Brisbane Tourism, Tel 3221 8411

Coral Sea, (Ken Harlands), Tel 0411 303 040

Customs House Brasserie, 399 Queen Street, City, Tel 3365 8921

Dental Hospital (Brisbane), Turbot Street (Cnr Albert Street) Brisbane 4000, Tel 3231 3777

Dental Hospital (Children's), Herston Road, Herston 4006, Tel 3253 1025

Didgeridoona Tel 5491 8797

Disability Services Unit Tel 3224 8031

Dockside Apartment Hotel,44 Ferry Street, Kangaroo Point, Q 4169, Tel 3891 6644

Dockside Marina (Ray Dahleen) 389 166 77/0418 772 080

Doggett Street Studio, 85 Doggett Street, Tel: 3252 9292

Dolfin Real Estate, Point Lookout, Tel 3409 8777

Dymocks, 239 Albert Street, Tel 3229 4266

e'cco, 100 Boundary and Adelaide streets, City, Tel 3831 8344

Ed and Mary's, cnr Mary and Edward Street Tel 3229 6607

Elision Ensemble, Tel 3365 7314

EMERGENCIES, Tel 000

Emergency Police Tel 3364 6464

Emporio, Eagle Street Pier, 1 Eagle Street, City, Tel 3229 9915

Enjoy Inn, cnr Duncan and Wickham Streets, Fortitude Valley Tel 3252 3838

Expressions Dance Co Tel 3210 0274

Fat Boys 321 Brunswick St (in the Mall), Tel 3252 3789

Fire-Works Gallery, 678 Ann Street, Fortitude Valley, Tel 3216 1250

Folio Books, 80 Albert Street, Tel 3221 1368

Fortitude Gallery, 164C Arthur Street, Tel 3254 2644

Fusions Gallery, Cnr Malt and Brunswick streets, Fortitude Valley, Tel 3358 5122

FW Canteen, 352 Brunswick Street, Fortitude Valley, Tel 3252 2956

Gail's, 210 Given Terrace, Paddington, Tel 3367 0398

Gallery 482, 482 Brunswick Street, Tel 3254 0933

Gallery Aesthete, 253 Moray Street, Tel 3358 1483

Gambaro's 33 and 34 Caxton Street, Petrie Terrace, Tel 3369 9500

Gay and Lesbian Welfare Association, Tel 3839 3277

Goodtime Surf and Sail 29 Ipswich Road Woolloongabba, Q 4102, Tel 3391 8588

Gourmet Haus Deli and Cafe in Racecourse Road, Ascot, Tel 3216 4899

Grand View Hotel, 49 North Street, Cleveland Point, Tel 3286 1002

Green Papaya, 898 Stanley Street, East Brisbane, Tel 3217 3599

Hamilton Hotel, South Drive, Hamilton, Tel 32268 7500

Have Chopsticks, Will Wander, Tel 3289 1919

Heritage, On the Botanic Gardens, Edward Street, Brisbane Q 4000, Toll free reservations: 1800 773 700

Hub Internet Cafe, 125 Margaret Street, 3229 1119

Il Centro, Eagle Street Pier, 1 Eagle Street,Tel 3221 6090

Indigo and Cactus, Shop 14 Elizabeth St Arcade, Tel 3211 2441

Indooroopilly Golf Club. Meiers Rd Indooroopilly, Tel 3870 2012

Inn on the Park, 507 Coronation Drive, Toowong. Tel 3870 9222,

Institute of Modern Art, 608 Ann Street, Tel 3252 5750

Interpreter Service (24 hours), 100 Edward Street, Tel 13 14 50

Isis Brasserie, 446 Brunswick Street, Fortitude Valley, Tel 3852 1155

Island Transport Services, Redland Bay, Tel 3829 0008

Jameson's Wine Bar, 475 Adelaide Street, Tel 3831 7633

Jan Murphy Gallery, Level 1, 482 Brunswick Street,Tel 3254 1855

Jazzworks, 54 Latrobe Terrace, Tel 3367 0985

John Oxley Library, Stanley Street, South Bank Tel 3840 7885

Jubilee Hotel, 470 St Paul's Terrace, Fortitude Valley, Tel 3252 4508

K2 Base Camp 140 Wickham St, Tel 3854 1340

Kadoya Shop 30 Elizabeth St Arcade, Tel 32293993

Khan's Kitchen, 75 Hardgrave Road, West End, Tel 3844 0877

King Ahiram's, 88 Vulture Street, West End, Tel 3846 1678

Kooemba Jdarra, 109 Edwards Street, Tel 3221 1660

La Boite, Tel 3369 1622

Larrikin 74 Worthing Rd Victoria Point Tel 3206 3523

Lasting Impressions, 6 Elizabeth Street, Kenilworth (074) 46 0422

Le Scoops, 283 Given Terrace, Paddington.Tel 3368 2640

Life-Line Counselling Service (24 hours), Tel 13 1114

Lighthouse Restaurant, 237 Shore Street, Cleveland Point, Tel 3286 5555

Malaysian Experience, 80 Jephson Street, Toowong, Tel 3870 2646

Manly Hotel, Cnr Cambridge Pde and Station Terrace, Manly,Tel 3396 8188

Marco Polo Restaurant Level 2, Treasury Casino, Queen Street, Tel 3306 8744

Mary Ryan 179 Latrobe Terrace, Paddington Tel 3368 1694; Brisbane

Arcade, Tel 3221 9922; New Farm,
Tel 3254 0444

Mater Misericordiae Hospital, Raymond
Terrace, South Brisbane 4104,
Tel 3840 8111

Medium Rare, 102 Kedron Road, North
Wilston, Tel 3856 5588

Michael's Riverside Restaurant, Riverside
Centre, 123 Eagle Street, Brisbane,
Tel 3832 5522

Mick's Nut Shop, 31 Hardgrave Street,
West End, Tel 3844 7396

Milburn Gallery, 100 Sydney Street, New
Farm, Tel 3254 0294

Morgan's Seafood, Bird O'Passage Parade,
Scarborough, Tel 3203 5744

Naturally Queensland , 160 Ann Street,
Tel 3227 8186

New Farm Art, 697 Brunswick Street,
Tel 3254 0954

New Farm Deli, 900 Brunswick St. New
Farm, Tel 3358 2634

New Wing Hing BBQ, 187 Wickham
Street, City, Tel 3252 4100

O'Reilly's, Tel 3821 0057

Opera Queensland, Tel, 3875 3030

OPG, Dana Cooper Tel 3257 0433

Outdoor Pursuits Group, Dana Cooper
Tel 3257 0433

Paddington Antique Centre, 167 Latrobe
Terrace, Tel 3369 8088

Paddy Pallin 138, Whickham St
Tel 3252 4408

Palace Backpackers, Cnr Ann & Edward
Streets, Brisbane Q 4000 Tel 3211 2433

Palace Cafe, Ann Street, City,
Tel 3211 9277

Pamela's Pantry 'Savoir Fair' Shop 6 Park
Rd, Milton, Tel 3368 1693

Philip Bacon Galleries, 2 Arthur Street,

Tel 3358 3555

Pier Nine Oyster Bar, Eagle Street Pier, 1
Eagle Street, City, Tel 3229 2194

Pine and Bamboo, 968 Wynnum Road,
Cannon Hill, Tel 3399 9095

Plotz Gallery, 49B James Street, Tel 3216
0123

Poulos Restoration Station, 98
Waterworks Road, Ashgrove,
Tel 3366 5855

Prince Charles Hospital, Rode Road,
Chermside 4032, Tel 3350 8111

Princess Alexandra Hospital, Ipswich
Road, Woolloongabba 4102,
Tel 3240 2111

QFMA Tel 3225 1848

QTTC (Queensland Tourist and Travel
Corporation), 123 Eagle Street, Brisbane
Q 4000, Tel 3406 5400

Quay West, 132 Alice Street, Brisbane Q
4000. Toll free reservations: 1800 672 726

Queen Elizabeth 11 Jubilee Hospital,
Kessels Road, Coopers Plains, Q 4108,
Tel 3275 6111

Queen Street Mall Information Centre,
corner Queen and Albert Streets,
Tel 3229 5918

Queens Arms Hotel, 64 James Street,
Teneriffe, Tel 3358 2799

Queensland Aids Council, 32 Peel Street,
City Tel 3844 1990

Queensland Art Gallery, Melbourne
Street, South Brisbane, Tel 3840 7303
  Art Gallery shop Tel 3840 7290

Queensland Ballet , Tel 3846 5266

Queensland Cyclist Association,
Tel 3390 1477

**Queensland Fisheries Management
Authority** (QFMA) Tel 3225 1848

Queensland Museum, South Bank,
Tel 3840 7635

Queensland Museum shop Tel 3840 7729

Queensland Performing Arts Complex
Show enquiries: Tel 3846 4444.Bookings
by telephone: Dial 'n' Charge Tel 3846
4646; FREECALL (outside Brisbane)
1800 777 699. TTY Tel 3840 7183.
Handling fee of $6.Bookings by mail:
Payable to Queensland Peforming Arts
Trust, plus $6 handling fee. Box Office,
PO Box 3567, South Bank, Q 4101.
Bookings by fax: Fax 3844 7790. Group
bookings: Tel 3840 7466.Disabilities
information, Tel 3840 7500.Free tours:
Depart ticket sales foyer, noon, Mon–Fri,
Tel 3840 7436. Promenade Cafe open
10am–4pm Mon–Sat on performance
nights. Alfresco dining, licensed. Lyrebird
Restaurant Lunch Mon-Sat, pre-theatre,
post-theatre suppers. Tel 3846 2434.

Queensland Performing Arts Trust, PO
Box 3567, South Brisbane Q 4101,
Tel 3840 7984

Queensland Rail TransInfo Line 13 1230

Queensland Symphony Orchestra,
Tel 3377 5000

Queensland Theatre Company,
Tel 3840 7000

Queensland University Bookshop (see
University of Queensland Bookshop)

Queensland Writers' Centre, 535
Wickham Terrace, Tel 3839 1243

Queensland Youth Orchestra Council,
Bridge Street, Fortitude Valley,
Tel 3257 1191

Rape/Incest Crisis Centre, Tel 3844 4008

Ray White Real Estate at Point Lookout,
Tel 3409 825

Red Books, 350a Brunswick Street,
Tel 3216 0747

Red Cross Tea Rooms Basement, Brisbane
City Hall, Adelaide Street, Tel 3403 8888

Redlands Tourism, PO Box 021 Cleveland

Q 4163 Tel 3821 0057

Ric's Cafe Bar, 321 Brunswick Street,
Fortitude Valley, Tel 3854 1772

Rock 'n' Roll Circus, Tel 3891 6163

Rock'n Roll Fruit and Deli, 500 Logan Rd,
Greenslopes, Tel 3394 3522

Rocklea Markets, Sherwood Road,
Rocklea, Tel 3379 1062

Romeo's, 216 Petrie Terrace, Tel 3367 0955

Rosalie Gourmet Market, cnr Baroona and
Nash Street Rosalie, Tel 3876 6222

Rosco Canoes, 388 Lutchwich Road
Windsor, Tel 3357 7465

Rosebank Cottage, 210 Mulgrave Road,
Red Hill, Tel 3367 1478

Royal Albert, Cnr Elizabeth and Albert
Streets (opposite Myer Centre)
Toll free reservations: 100 655 054.

**Royal Automobile Club of Queensland
(RACQ)**, Tel 3361 2444

Royal Brisbane Hospital, Herston Road,
Herston 4006 Tel 3253 8111

Royal Children's Hospital, Herston Road,
Herston 4006, Tel 3253 3777

Royal Exchange 10 High Street, Toowong,
Tel 3371 2555

Royal Queensland Golf Club, West Curtin
Ave, Eagle Farm, Tel 3268 1127

Rudds' Pub, Nobby, Tel 0746 963 211

Salvo Careline (Salvation Army),
Tel 1300 363 622

Satay Club Cafe, 66 Charlotte Street, City,
Tel 3229 8855

Savode, 11 Stratton Street, Tel 3852 2870

Schonell Twin Cinema, Tel 3321 7690

Sciencentre, Tel 3220 0166

Scout Outdoor Center, 132 Wickham
Street, 3252 4744

Senso Unico, 92-96 Merthyr Road, New
Farm, Tel 3358 6644

Serious Persuits, Angela Ramsay, 99

Cubberla Street, Fig Tree Pocket, Q 4069, Tel 015 027 597

Sheil Collection, 202 Edward Street, Brisbane, Tel 3221 4881

Shingle Inn, 254 Edward Street, Tel 3221 9039

Siggi's at the Port Office, Heritage Hotel, Edward Street, Tel 3221 4555

Skate Biz, 101 Albert Street, Tel 3220 0157

Skateboarding info:Tel 3403 6757

South Bank Butterfly House, Tel 3844 1112

South Brisbane Dental Hospital, Main Street, Woolloongabba, 4102 Tel 3391 3754

St Lucia Golf Links Cnr Indooroopilly Rd and Carawa Street, Indooroopilly, Tel 3403 2557

State Library of Queensland shop Tel 3840 7900

Stradbroke Ferries, Toondah Harbour, Middle Street, Cleveland Tel 3286 2666

Sweethearts Cafe, 161 Latrobe Terrace, Tel 3369 5193

Swiss in West End, 181 Boundary St West End, Tel 39442937

Tables of Toowong, 88 Miskin Street, Toowong, Tel 3371 4558

Tandems, Info: 015 123 037

Taylor's Damn Fine Bed and Breakfast, Eumundi, Tel (075) 442 8685

The Grape, 1st Floor, 308 Wickham Street, Fortitude Valley, Tel 3852 1301

The Malaysian Experience 80 Jephson Street, Toowong, Tel 3870 2646

The Rest, 20 Latrobe Terrace, Tel 3369 8086

The Ritz, Musgrave Street and Windsor Street, Tel 3876 3665.

The Travellers' Medical Service, 245 Albert Street, Tel 3211 3611

Thornbury House,1 Thornbury Street, Spring Hill, Tel 3832 5985

Tibetian Kichen, 454 Brunswick St Valley Tel 3358 5906

Tognini's, Baroona Road Shopping Village, Milton, Tel 33690915

Tourism Brisbane (see Brisbane Tourism)

TransInfo 13 12 30

Transit Centre Information Office, Tel 3236 2020.

Trattoria di Santa Patata, BYO, 19 Claxton Street, Tel 3217 6920

Traveller's Medical Service, 5th floor Coles building, 210 Queen Street, Tel 3221 8083

Two Small Rooms, 517 Milton Road, Toowong, Tel 3371 5251

University of Queensland Bookshop Staff House Rd, St Lucia campus, Tel 3365 2168; Fax 3365 1977

Urban Reef Seafood Takeaway, Shop 6 Teneriffe Village, cnr Macquarie and Florence streets, Tel 3257 2588

Waverley Paddington B&B, 5 Latrobe Terrace, Paddington Q 4064 Tel 3369 8973

Wickham Hotel, 308 Wickham Hotel, Tel 3852 1301

Wild Adventure Sportz, 3/243 Edward Street Brisbane Tel 3221 5747

Women's Infolink counselling service, Tel 3229 1580 or Freecall 1800 177 577

Wonga Villa,194 Bonney Avenue, Clayfield Tel/Fax: 3862 2183

Yatala Pes, Macphersons Road, Yatala, Tel 3287 2468

Yellow Submarine, 66 Quay Street, City, Tel: 3211 3424

Yen, Anna Tel 3846 1651-*-

Youth Emergency Services Inc, Tel 3357 7655

ORDER FORM

FREE UPDATES

1. On the Internet (Australia and international)

All Untourist travel guides are updated weekly. This information is available 24 hours a day, free of charge on our web site **www.untourist.com.au**

2. By mail (Australia only)

At any time six months after the print date of *UnTourist Brisbane*, you can get your free mailed update by simply sending this order form (copied if you like) to us in a stamped, self-addressed envelope.

UNTOURIST GUIDE BOOKS

I would like a copy of the latest edition of:
(please tick box)

❑ Untourist Sydney $29.95 ea

❑ Untourist Tasmania $29.95 ea

❑ Untourist Brisane $29.95 ea

Please debit my credit card (add $10 for outside Australia for up to 2 books). (Visa, Bankcard or Mastercard only)
Amount: $AUD_____

❑❑❑❑ ❑❑❑❑ ❑❑❑❑ ❑❑❑❑

EXPIRY DATE_____ SIGNATURE _____

NAME _____

ADDRESS _____

_____

NOTE: If you are buying books, you need not include the stamped, self-adressed envelope for your updates. ❑ I would also like Untourist Brisbane updates.
SEND COMPLETED FORM TO: UnTourist Co PO Box 209 Balmain NSW 2041
Australia/**Fax (02) 9974 1396**   e-mail: **info@untourist.com.au**

Have you seen our other Untourist books?
Here is what the reviewers say about them:

"SMH: *"The truth about Sydney from the savvy locals – picks up where the other guide books stop."*

Gourmet Traveller: *"Impeccably researched, immaculately presented"*

Australian: *"Recommended for travellers not tourists."*

The Age: *"If only I'd had [Untourist Sydney] when visiting Sydney."*

The Bulletin: *"What a relief to see something that is both innovative and useful"*

Adelaide Advertiser: *"Full marks for Untourist Tasmania – if you are headed for Tasmania, stow this in your luggage".*

News-Mail *".....for travellers like me who shudder at being labelled a 'tourist' that Untourist Tasmania is aimed."*

UNTOURIST TASMANIA, by Suzanne Baker. It's more than a book – it's a package of information – 155 pages with the best things to do, see, eat, buy and the best places to stay. Ring-bound and comes in a full colour folder which also holds a sturdy, full-colour travel map of Tasmania, plus a wilderness facilities guide and map.

UNTOURIST SYDNEY, by Jacqueline Huie. Now a best-seller, it is the first discerning, in-depth guide to one of the great resort cities of the world.

IN THE PIPELINE

Untourist Queensland, by Baker/Huie guide you around the Sunshine State, picking out all the best bits and leaving the rest for the tourists. Ready for launch.

Untourist Sydney Plus, by Jacqueline Huie. An updated and expanded edition of Untourist Sydney incorporating the best of New South Wales.

Untourist Victoria, will uncover the best places to stay and all the secret joys that never get into the tourist brochures.

ORDER FORM – SEE OVER PAGE